THE
SECURE
CiO

CLAIRE PALES

First published 2018 for Claire Pales by

LONGUEVILLE
MEDIA

Longueville Media Pty Ltd
PO Box 205
Haberfield NSW 2045 Australia
www.longmedia.com.au
info@longmedia.com.au
Tel. +61 410 519 685

A CIP catalogue record for this book is available from the National Library of Australia website: www.nla.gov.au

ISBN: 978-0-6482047-9-4

THE
SECURE
CiO

HOW TO HIRE AND RETAIN GREAT
CYBER SECURITY TALENT TO
PROTECT YOUR ORGANISATION

CLAIRE PALES

THE
SECURE
CIO

Claire Pales is the Director of 27 Lanterns, a consulting company committed to helping organisations create and sustain effective information security teams. For the past 15 years, Claire has gained experience establishing teams and leading award-winning security strategies throughout Australia and Asia including Hong Kong, China and India. Claire's information and cyber security experience spans critical infrastructure, online and ecommerce teams, with an ongoing focus to grow and coach information security professionals from graduates to leaders and help businesses to establish exceptional information security practices.

Claire has a Bachelors Degree in Police Studies, Post-Graduate studies in e-Crime Investigation and executive coaching qualifications.

Based in Melbourne, Claire has four children, is a regular industry blogger and actively volunteers with the Australian Women in Security Network.

www.27lanterns.com.au

Testimonials

"Claire successfully blends her corporate, consulting and global expertise to offer an insightful and pragmatic approach to information and cyber security. Her independence is a draw card for clients as Claire provides objective recommendations which gain confidence with executives and Boards. Claire's ability to build relationships and trust allows her to gain insights and deliver value sooner." – **Anna Leibel, Executive Manager, Technology at UniSuper**

"There can be no doubt that this connected world presents some of the most challenging risks and brilliant opportunities. Securing an organisation so that its cyber security settings are appropriate is an issue that confronts all organisations- both big and small. The second biggest challenge in cyber security is how to find the right cyber security professional.

Claire's book is not only full of her insights which she has accumulated from years of experience but it is perfectly timed as the marketplace is awash with opportunities for security professionals. She not only addresses the importance of selecting the right cyber security 'warrior' but also provides readers with an enduring framework so that organisations, particularly their CIOs, understand that, with the right controls, culture and expectations, cyber security is a risk that cannot be eliminated but can be effectively managed. This is definitely a cyber page-turner!" – **Rachael Falk, Cyber Security Adviser, Pace & Scale Pty Ltd**

"From the very moment we connected with Claire, we knew she was the perfect fit to guide us in our cyber security journey. Aside from being an experienced, well respected and extremely passionate Information Security professional, Claire understands what makes individuals and organisations tick. Claire's ability to combine technical expertise with an understanding of how to drive organisational change is a wonderful asset. May this book inspire many others to follow in her footsteps". – **John Finnan, Head of Payment Operations and Group ICT at MYOB**

"Claire is unique within the infosecurity industry. Someone you can give almost any challenge and trust that she will get it done well and with the utmost professionalism. She is an inspiring speaker, writer and coach.

We have been absolutely privileged to have her as our AWSN National Events Coordinator and Melbourne events manager for the past 12 months where she has helped organise CSO roadshows across Australia and NZ, Gartner panels and local events. She has been an incredible coach who has helped me through many crises." – **Jacqui Loustau – Founder, Australian Women in Security Network**

Contents

Introduction

'In [the cyber security industry], we have zero unemployment and the demand is massive.'

Craig Davies
CEO, Australian Cyber Security Growth Network

As a nation, we are not on top of the threat of cyber-attack. And we are not the only ones globally to face an uncertain future when it comes to protecting our businesses in the digital age. Recent newsworthy events have proven we are ill-equipped and underprepared for the onslaught of cyber events and incidents that impact our organisations daily.

In the past year, business lost more than $20 million due simply to virus emails, a 230% increase on the $8.6 million lost in the 2016–17 financial year.[1] Australian businesses are looking to prevent future cyberattacks similar to the recent *WannaCry* and *Petya* ransomware viruses, which locked computer systems and demanded a ransom before files would be unlocked. No organisation is immune – even companies trusted with guarding our nation's biggest secrets, such as the Australian Signals Directorate, were caught up in the 47,000 local cybercrime incidents identified by the Australian Cyber Security Centre in the past year, which comprised everything from data breaches to state-sponsored hacking.

Cyber criminals are faster, more efficient, and one step ahead of most of our efforts to minimise risk and arm our businesses against their assault – targeted, opportunistic, or otherwise.

If you're reading this, there's a good chance your board, audit and risk committees, or chief executive, has read of the above activity and is starting to ask questions. There's a good chance you've been tasked with doing something about the cyber threat that your organisation has identified as a result of the heightened global awareness. And usually part of doing something involves employing a dedicated security leader to protect your organisation and appease your board with confidence and certainty when it comes to cyber security.

If this is where you are at, you're in luck. There are some incredible security leaders in the world who are passionate, driven, and focused individuals who maintain high integrity no matter whose apple cart they upset. But, they won't take on just any job or help just any organisation, and because of the current threat landscape, they are choosy about how their expertise is utilised. Their skills are highly sought after, competition is fierce, and salaries (especially in Australia) are on the rise in order to attract the best.

So, how to do you find and retain these security warriors? This book addresses this question. It's about digging deep, planning ahead, and maybe taking a chance on someone who doesn't have it all but may have a lot of what your organisation needs. If no one had taken a chance on me, I wouldn't be writing this book now.

When I started out in the late 1990s, cyber security was not on my professional radar. Two years after leaving university, with my career drive and purpose at full speed, I met the head of corporate security at Telstra and asked her out for coffee. Six months later I was working for her, and I spent the next few years giving court evidence for the police and government agencies on behalf of Telstra across the country, from regional courthouses to the federal court.

I worked hard, took loads of advice, studied further, and raised my profile as I became more and more passionate about working in this space. After more than 15 years in the industry, I now work for myself. I've built teams, led award-winning strategies, and helped protect organisations in Asia and Australia from cyber-attack. My years as a leader in cyber and information security have brought me to today, sharing my experience and passion for helping businesses institute exceptional security practices and establish in-house security leadership.

Who is this book for?

The Secure CIO is written for chief information officers (CIOs) who have cyber or information security staff reporting to them, or would like to.

Despite more c-level roles becoming available in security, most security leaders and various other security roles still report to the CIO. The cyber security job market is increasingly difficult for hiring managers and candidates to navigate. Many roles sit vacant for months, which causes more stress for CIOs, on top of their mounting workload, and increases the risk to the organisation. Finding and retaining the right security staff gives CIOs a level of certainty that cannot otherwise be assured. To have an in-house expert and leader assessing and addressing cyber risk before (and after) it materialises can change the direction of a business for the better.

Why did I write this book?

The Secure CIO meets the demand for advice and reassurance about the effective hiring of leaders to address cyber security risk.

Research by the Australian Information Security Association shows that the perceived cyber security skills shortage in Australia is fuelled by management's lack of understanding of the risks.

This book is structured first to provide insights to you, the CIO, about common mistakes made when hiring cyber security leaders. This is followed by a five-step framework, from setting your agenda to finding that strategic employee who meets the needs of the organisation. It responds to the key problems of how to attract quality candidates, concern about the expertise needed to assess a candidate's security skills, and how to reduce board and stakeholder pressure to address cyber risk.

The problem

In my research, it was often noted by CIOs that the directive to recruit a security leader was based on a desire to combat the global security threats. Boards, audit and risk committees, chief executives, and sometimes previous CIOs often requested this new leadership position without understanding what skills were required, the company's security position, and how to find good security staff who would stay.

What prevents CIOs from hiring and retaining the cyber security talent their organisation needs? Common problems include:

- Failing to identify what is needed before handing the hiring to a human resources manager or recruiter
- Basing the job description on what the organisation wants, not what it needs
- Seeking a candidate who can perform more than the role of one person
- Job descriptions that are written by people who aren't familiar with what securing the organisation would entail and which are not linked to the business strategy
- Pressure from the board and other stakeholders for CIOs to address cyber risk so they can appease shareholders and customers

Once the job is advertised, further issues arise:

- The ad does not attract quality, qualified candidates
- The candidate may have the right cultural fit but the interviewer is unsure of his or her technical skills
- Expectations of the candidates are unclear
- Candidates are strong in some areas but have no skill in others

The five-step framework for effective hiring

How do we overcome this long list of issues and concerns? The following framework will help you set appropriate expectations for the role and then assess candidates' skills:

1. **Clarity – establish your agenda**

   What is the state of security in your organisation from your perspective and that of your stakeholders, and how does that affect the person you hire?

2. **Compass – what direction do you want the role to take?**

   Based on your agenda, what are your expectations of this person and what skills does your organisation need now?

3. **Connection – how to hire**

   From the initial search through to the interview stage and offering a candidate the role.

4. **Commitment – committing to a candidate**

   Once the candidate has accepted your offer, what support do they need?

5. **Coaching – settling your new staff member into the organisation**

   When your recruit starts, brief them on the agenda, reiterate expectations and set goals. Provide coaching and mentoring support for a smoother transition to the role.

Following the framework to hire a head of information security will provide you and the board with that certainty that you have a new expert on board whose role is to:

- ensure cyber security is taken seriously
- protect the consumers of your product or services
- define a clear strategy to manage your cyber security activities and invest in the areas that matter most
- focus on preventing, detecting, and responding to incidents, and confer with the audit and risk committees that cyber risk is being handled appropriately
- collaborate, influence, and inspire.

So, how to establish this certainty?

The Dilemma

'Most people spend more time and energy going around problems than in trying to solve them.'

Henry Ford, *founder, Ford Motor Company*

This section provides some insights about common problems for CIOs when hiring cyber security leaders. Looking at job ads for roles that have remained unfilled for long periods, and at the hundreds of applications sent to recruiters who are not suitable for the role, I have found three recurring problems:

1. Security is considered an IT problem

The responsibility to hire an expert and manage security is still considered an IT issue and usually the responsibility of the CIO. Their ability to assess candidates varies considerably, and unless they are clear about what they're after, it may take a long time to fill the role.

CIOs have a complex and diverse set of responsibilities. They need to consider the strategies of every division of the company. They must take risks to drive innovation, but at the same time, focus on risk mitigation to deliver on security needs. This can create conflict in the CIO's mind about looking after the needs of the business and the customer. To do this they need a strong team of advisers to lead and educate them about new ways to achieve business goals.

An extra challenge for the CIO, if security is a new responsibility, is that initially a budget to manage security may need to be 'found' among other IT funds. A simple phishing test subscription can set you back $50,000 a year, and not many IT budgets have that lying around, let alone larger sums for security monitoring, or the staff to act on incident alerts or risk assessment results. The average security budget for a mid-tier organisation is in the hundreds of thousands of dollars, so taking this kind of money from another initiative or priority will be felt on the bottom line.

The SANS Institute is the largest IT security training, certification, and security documents source in the world. Their *Security Spending Trends Report* for 2016 found that since 2014, security usually accounts for 4–6% of a company's total IT budget. But the number of companies with budgets in the 10–12% range is growing.[2]

As the need for security spending increases, however, overall IT budgets appear to be dropping, with mid-tier organisations being in the range of US$1 million–10 million.[3]

And speaking of expenditure, who pays to clean up a security breach? The Australian Cyber Security Centre says, 'The costs of compromise are almost certainly more expensive than preventative measures',[4] and therefore having a dedicate security budget (not one scrapped together) for things such as early incident detection is becoming key to protecting your organisation.

2. Your organisation is unable to attract quality candidates

This is often due to an excessively broad job description, requiring that one person play the role of many, and perform more than one security function.

The skills required for a head of information security, or indeed a chief information security officer, are unlikely to match those of someone who needs to review code or assess the technical specifications of a new security product. I'm not saying that senior leaders wouldn't have the skills or background to do this, but it's unlikely this is how they want to spend their days. Furthermore, their technical skills may be outdated if they have been in management for some time rather than in hands-on roles.

Giving the new security leader the responsibility of many roles may occur because the organisation hasn't previously had a cyber risk person, or there is funding for only one position at this time.

Some security leaders will take this in their stride and agree to a larger workload if they know respite is coming. But leaders who fit the job and culture requirements and can achieve multi-level results with such a workload are rare.

To attract the right candidates, the job description should reflect the reality (needs), not the dream outcome (wants). By all means decide on some non-negotiable traits and experience. Be clear on what this person needs to achieve and what the priorities are.

3. Board pressure

There is board pressure to fill the role and have someone address cyber risk fast.

It's important for the board to voice its concerns about cyber security so you are aware of its position; however, panic and knee-jerk reactions are not helpful. The Australian Cyber Security Centre found that regular board and senior management level discussions about security are a key factor distinguishing cyber-resilient organisations from less resilient ones.[5]

While the board should see cyber security as everyone's responsibility, they will still want one confident, trusted voice to assure them that security is being addressed. It is important to set expectations about the timeframe required to fill this security role.

Addressing these three recurring problems brought me to the central question that is answered by this book: **How can you find and retain a great cyber security leader to give the board certainty and protect the organisation?**

Section 1

Clarity: Establishing your Agenda

'Preparation is the key to success.'

Alexander Graham Bell, *inventor, innovator*

The framework begins with clarity – clarity on why you are recruiting, on the current state of security in your organisation from your perspective and that of your stakeholders, and on where a new leader would fit into the overall organisational structure.

How many businesses take the time before recruitment begins to understand their security position, the skills the business needs, and what value can be added through a security role? From the jobseeker's perspective of available roles, how many candidates truly know what they are getting themselves into if they are successful?

Securing your business can be overwhelming, especially when starting from scratch. Once your organisation has identified a need to make security part of the way you do business, how do you get started? Should you go big and seek a deep-dive risk assessment? Should you consider a three-year strategic implementation? Should you hire a head of information security?

What is the best approach to help you identify what information security looks like at your company? Instead of a 'go big' approach, like those mentioned above, organisations could begin by asking key people in the business what security means to them, what they expect from a security program, how security would align with their business strategy, and given all the competing priorities, where a security program would fit in their organisation. I can feel you rolling your eyes as you imagine these security-related conversations with the CEO, the marketing guy and the under-the-pump head of IT ops. But having someone draw opinions, information, and aspirations from every corner of the organisation to answer the difficult questions can establish the true value placed on security by those in the driver's seat.

We have learnt that telling leaders, engineers, and anyone who will listen what security looks like is often met with groans, reluctant compliance, or panic. If we gave the business the opportunity to say what it thinks about security – and what it knows about security, which is often only what it sees in the media – this information starts to form a foundation on which incoming security leaders can build their roadmap, to know who else will champion security, and to establish what information security success means for your organisation.

Starting by establishing your organisation's security agenda will help your future team to align to your business's priorities. Yes, there will be some difficult conversations and uncomfortable silences, but won't they be worth it, if it means agreeing to a way forward together?

1

The state of the industry

'The conversation around cyber security is changing – risks are better understood and opportunities better realised.'

Cyber security roundtable meeting online news report,
24 April 2017, Dept. of the Prime Minister and Cabinet, Australia

In Australia, there is a growing, unified front towards combating cyber security risk as part of protecting our borders – virtual and otherwise.

In business, the growing number of conversations about cyber is helping to prepare organisations for potential cyber threats. In a government survey, 81% of organisations recognise that all staff have responsibility for ensuring cyber security and, overall 73% regularly discuss cyber security at the most senior management levels.[6] A move towards more senior security leaders who can approach the board with confidence and give its members certainty has become a must for cyber-resilient organisations.

Businesses, however, are finding security leaders hard to come by, and the changing face of the industry is more demanding than ever. The following numbers demonstrate some of the challenges:

- At any time, there are 350,000 open roles for cyber security professionals in the U.S.[7]
- 78% of AISA members surveyed believe that lack of clarity about skills required contributes to difficulties in recruiting for cyber security roles.[8]

- Difficulties in recruiting because of wage restrictions and the tendency to leave positions unfilled are consistent with evidence of the limited growth of cyber security teams; 52% reported that their team had remained about the same or grown by less than 10%, while more than 11% of respondents reported a decrease.[9]
- Australia will likely need about 11,000 additional cyber security workers over the next decade – for technical as well as non-technical positions – just to meet the industry's 'business-as-usual' demand forecasts.[10]

These statistics alone can make attempts to hire cyber security staff daunting, and almost feel pointless. But more and more research is being produced which informs governments, universities, and enterprises of the changes they can make to better meet the cyber security needs of our country and the world. Some of the actions that can be taken are to:

- Attract, train and retain more women (more on this in chapter 6). At only 11% of the cyber security workforce (and yet 48% of the general workforce),[11] more women would contribute to this great industry, if only they knew about it.
- Collaborate; get involved. Enterprises, academia and government need to work together to educate the community on the need for more cyber security professionals.
- Address ongoing development, as well as access to mentors and sponsors, which is critical to attracting, developing, and retaining professionals in the cyber security workforce.

Key takeaway

We have never been more aware of the perceived gap between organisational expectations and available cyber security skills. There are many opportunities to address this gap: by identifying and mentoring the next generation of leaders, speaking up about the importance of cyber security, and playing our part in attracting the best and brightest to the industry.

2

What is your why?

'If you hire people just because they can do a job, they'll work for your money.

But if you hire people who believe what you believe, they'll work for you with blood, sweat and tears.'

Simon Sinek, *author*

When I began asking CIOs what problem they were solving by hiring a security professional, the answers didn't surprise me.

Responses such as 'The audit and risk committee told us a recent audit showed we need to address cyber risk better, and this included hiring a leader to take responsibility' were common. Some responses focused on domain expertise, having an expert to define the strategy and mitigate the organisation's security risks.

Some of the less common responses were that a security leader was needed to advise the CIO and that security awareness was key to their remit.

The overwhelming majority spoke about protecting the customer. This is a great place to start as a rationale for having a security team and a security leader. If you put protecting your customer at the heart of what you do, your reason for being will be similar to that of the sales, marketing, finance, and operations teams: retaining the customer. Protecting the customer also means retaining your reputation in the market and ensuring the resilience of systems to continue operating through threats and incidents.

The point of this chapter is that no matter what your reasons are for bringing in a security leader, you are prepared to back this leader in their pursuits to deliver.

You don't want to hire a scapegoat. You don't want to hire one person to do the job of many, and you don't want to hire a security leader so the organisation can wear it as a badge of good corporate citizenship. Hiring a security leader takes work, some of which needs to be done before they arrive. Understanding what you need them to do, what they will be stepping into, and how you plan to support them emotionally, financially, and organisationally is incredibly important. Yes, these leaders are grown-ups; it's not their first security gig (in most cases) and they can probably get the motor running themselves within the first few weeks. However, if you have done the hard thinking, understand where the organisation is at (and not just through audit findings), and you have considered the impact this new leader will have on your organisation, positive and negative for some, you and the other c-level leaders will also benefit.

I can hear you thinking, 'But isn't that what I'm hiring a security leader for, to do the hard thinking, to understand where the organisation is at, and to have a positive impact on the organisation?'

Yes. But if no one has agreed on expectations before the leader arrives, even if they are a replacement leader, there will be months of confusion, constant knockbacks for funding, and a great deal of frustration. Companies often excitedly bring in permanent security staff without considering where the team is coming from (or going) and what outcome they require.

Asking new staff to come in and 'make it secure' isn't enough to entice qualified security people from jobs where they are valued. Without knowing how the business got to where it is today, and what the path ahead looks like, it is impossible to recruit effectively for security-related roles. This forces some hiring managers to seek candidates who are more senior or specialist than is required, with possibly a bigger price tag than is necessary. Companies with clearly articulated security goals can give candidates an understanding of the value they can bring by joining the business. This also creates opportunities to seek candidates without traditional security backgrounds who may offer skills that better align with the required business outcomes.

It's your responsibility to see the job vacancy as more than purely filling a role. There is nothing more frustrating than beginning a job in security only to find that before you can deliver any results, you must first justify your existence. Companies define a bigger picture for marketing or product development, and security is no different. No matter whether it's a simple strategy or detailed roadmap, clear commitment to more than just security staffing leads to a sustainable security function and less likely attrition. The detail may change over time. but if hiring managers have enough information to be honest with themselves about why they are hiring, and honest with the candidate about the near- to medium-term expectations, incoming security staff will have a sense of their fit with the security culture and the priorities of the employer. With this in mind, why are some organisations not forward thinking about a better story to attract and retain the right security people?

Key takeaway

Decide on your why. Make sure that no matter why you're bringing in a security leader, you are prepared to back them in their pursuits to deliver against your rationale, agenda, and future strategy.

3

Security maturity

'Seek first to understand, and then be understood.'

Stephen Covey, *The 7 Habits of Highly Effective People*

I have been fortunate in my career to arrive in roles that have strategies – or the bones of one – already thought through. I then take the time to review the documentation and ensure the strategy fits the business, is up to date with the business strategy, is realistic, and is one I can be proud to deliver. As a new leader coming into an organisation, it gave me great confidence that in the absence of a security leader or team, an organisation had invested in understanding their security maturity and what they might need to do to improve. This was certainly a 'pro' when it came to deciding which roles to take on.

Of course, there are security leaders – leaders in all professions – who like to write and seek endorsement for their own strategies, end to end. This is fantastic. Even if the new leader wants to create their own roadmap, any documentation the organisation can provide, including reviews and literature, helps in the strategy planning process. Context, politics, documentation, and stakeholder opinions are vital artefacts.

Existing strategies will always be affected by those who deliver them, and on occasion I have made changes to ensure we were taking the organisation's security in a relevant direction. Also, my strengths lie in security awareness, leadership, and communication with all levels of the organisation. If any strategy missed these key elements, I ensured that communication outside of the security and IT teams was planned for and achieved.

Any new leader wants to make their mark on the organisation. How they do that will be up to them. But arriving to some form of plan helps guide the incoming leader as to the organisation's security risk and what fires need to be put out first.

This needn't involve extensive time and financial investment. Most CIOs, with some guidance from this book, can ascertain the organisation's high-level concerns. At the interview stage, ensure you provide enough insight for a new security leader to know what they are stepping into and what quick wins they can concentrate on.

I call these areas the 'big rocks'. Stephen Covey talks about the big rocks of life, and the idea comes from him. In essence, the big rocks are points of focus, areas to address that make the biggest impact. There will always be room for 'sand and pebbles', but addressing the big rocks takes away a large percentage of the security pain your organisation may be feeling.

The next couple of chapters will help you to understand how to identify these big rocks, of which I would recommend having three. In many cases, they become clear quite quickly. Here are some examples gleaned from experience and also through interviews with CIOs. The list is by no means exhaustive.

In a start-up:
The focus for the security leader may be on vendor management, application security, security of third party engagements, and basic network security. It's less likely to be about compliance and audit.

In a newly digital organisation:
Application security, incident response, security awareness, and cloud security may be the big rocks.

In a utility:
Big rocks could be defined as understanding IT and OT (operational technology) security, security awareness, and security monitoring/incident response.

The Agenda

The big rocks form the major part of the agenda. The agenda is not a strategy. I repeat, the agenda is not a strategy. The agenda sets the scene for the new leader and provides some facts, opinion, and context to which they can anchor in their first few months. The agenda forms the major part of the handover documents for the new leader (discussed in chapter 17). Imagine joining an organisation as a chief financial officer and no one giving you any idea of the financial state of the company. You have no staff, no background, just some outdated policies and full accountability to keep the organisation financially secure. This is what security people face every day, and if we could work towards giving them an agenda on which they can get off to a brisk start, this benefits not only the new leader but some of their peers.

Handing the new security leader a wad of audit reports is not the same as providing them with a security agenda. It serves a much different purpose. While audit reports provide important background and clarity on the key risks and the remediation recommended, they cannot replace an agenda that has been created with more than compliance in mind.

The agenda can cover details of interviews with leaders; a reflection of security against the values, mission, and strategic direction of the organisation; details of the current state of security and what is already in place (policies or technical controls); the big rocks; the opinions of leaders about the type of security leader needed and some valuable activities the new leader could kick off in line with the three big rocks.

The agenda plays one more role. If the direction to hire a new head of cyber or information security has been handed down from an audit and risk committee, or the board, the agenda shows that action has and will be taken immediately to begin addressing the security risk. While waiting for a new security leader to arrive, conducting interviews and gathering information have already started the conversation within the organisation. Stakeholders will know change is coming and that they are contributing to that change. Facts uncovered may lead to work that can be carried out immediately by a technical staff member or contractor. Life can go on while recruitment takes place, and any progress towards a more secure organisation can be reported to the board/committee until the new leader arrives. And when they do arrive, regular, engaging strategic updates to the board and executive are key. This way, when incidents happen unexpectedly, the board is already aware of the head of information security and the progress made towards improving security.

Key takeaway

The agenda provides a set of relevant facts regarding the security status of the organisation. While it is not a strategy, audit, or risk assessment, it pulls together details for the new leader to review. Understanding what the big rocks are, and what led to their identification, helps give the new leader some context and provides them with a strategic starting point.

4

What others are saying, Part 1

'It is wiser to find out than to suppose.'

Mark Twain, *writer and entrepreneur*

One of the main activities that will boil your agenda down to the big rocks is establishing how your leadership team (and other key stakeholders) see security within your organisation. This isn't simply chatting with them over coffee about their general thoughts. This is asking each of them pertinent questions to establish themes and inconsistencies of thought. These discussions/interviews take place with the executive leaders and with staff. Such staff may include, but not be limited to, consultants, contractors, and permanent employees who are the custodians of systems, data, and information relevant to security threats and risks.

The questions you ask will differ from organisation to organisation and depend on your 'security maturity'. The questions help to identify where the major gaps are and where you will gain the most support. For example, if the CEO doesn't see cyber as a risk but all the other leaders do, the troops you need to rally will be very different from the HR department or the developers.

As CIO, you have a lot of leverage, and you likely have quite specialised relationships with the leadership team. This can work for and against you when asking these questions. You may need to set some parameters before the conversation starts to ensure there is open, honest feedback. Or you could simply ask someone else who is more impartial to ask the questions on your behalf.

Either way, you want raw, specific data that helps to establish what your focus should be and what sort of security leader will be needed now and in the near future. I say 'near' because the security leader you need today is very different from the one you'll need in two years' time, because cyber changes quickly. And in two years' time, a lot of what will keep your leader busy will look different to when they arrived, especially if they begin their life with your organisation as the sole security operator. (More on that later.)

Here are some questions you might want to consider. They are in no particular order and only you can decide if they are relevant or whether you need to ask something different to identify the 'big rocks'.

- What do you believe a head of information security or a chief information security officer would be responsible for?
- Where do you see security fitting into the overall business strategy? (This is somewhat of a trick question. You hope security will be described not as a strategic pillar but as a foundation stone of the way the business operates – like culture and values. (As a side note, I have seen organisations who were not mature enough to 'lay' the foundation stone, and needed the strategic objective first before security became a way of doing business).
- What do you see as the organisation's biggest/No. 1 risk? It can be whatever you believe is the biggest risk, not necessarily a security-related one.
- How do you think the business will react to a more secure overlay in projects and in direction?
- What security practices are specific to your department (if any), and are they effective? (Some won't know the answer to this question, which demonstrates the need to communicate and implement the policies that are likely gathering dust somewhere.)

- Who has ultimate responsibility for security? (This will tell you how security would be seen should a major breach or other security incident occur).
- Who should we be educating first, customers or employees?
- Do you see security as a market differentiator?
- Who should a new security leader report to? (While the CIO is often the natural choice, sometimes it's the CFO, the CEO, the chief risk officer, the chief technology officer, or perhaps not even a c-level executive).
- What traits or attributes would you expect the leader to have? (This will tell you about the environment this new leader is stepping into. An influencer, an inspirer, a risk-taker, someone who is autonomous, resourceful, technically aware, or technically skilled – different types of skills and experience that might help a leader succeed.)
- How is change managed in the organisation?
- Who else would you recommend I speak to and raise these questions with? (The conversation may lead to names of people you hadn't considered).

Send any new questions or concerns that don't appear here that you would like to discuss to me at info@27lanterns.com. This also helps us to help others with fresh, new examples to consider.

One thing that has become clear to me in conducting these interviews is that common threads appear. In one organisation, of the 20 leaders and stakeholders I interviewed, 15 said that security in their organisation was too reactive, and that they felt they needed to be more proactive in order to see change. It became clear that they wanted more visibility of security, and to prevent incidents rather than respond to them. Another business I worked with were aligned on the premise that the CEO had ultimate responsibility for security, but that he wouldn't be aware of this; neither would he know what this responsibility required of him.

This feedback can be presented to the board, the executive, the audit committee – anyone who will listen. The answers to these questions are also gold for the incoming leader. Knowing how security is seen within the organisation, and how the leaders see security can be leveraged, is important. In a recent delivery of the framework, I read my interview records aloud to an incoming head of cyber security to help frame the organisation for them. I kept the conversation light and elaborated on my shorthand so that she could gain the most value from having the opinions broken down. The insight she took was overwhelming. She could relate to many of the stakeholders when meeting them face to face, having understood some of their concerns and ideas for spreading security awareness.

Key takeaway

In life, what others think isn't always important. But in security, knowing who will be backing you from day one, and who will be a challenge to win over, can make or break the security program – and the leader and their tenure. Sometimes, the most important insights come from the most unlikely places. Hearing what stakeholders say about security and risk may unearth some valuable actions to hitch to your agenda – and those responsible for implementing it. Target as many relevant people as time permits to ensure you have a good cross section of the organisation.

5

Aligning to business strategy

'Thinking of cyber security solely as an IT issue is like believing that a company's entire workforce, from the CEO down, is an HR issue.'

Steven Chabinsky, *global chair, Data, Privacy & Cybersecurity, White & Case*

If you have read chapter 2, you will know that the agenda is not meant to be a strategy in itself. The agenda is a starting point. Aligning your agenda to the overall business strategy is important. By this I don't mean including security in the strategy (see chapter 2 for a little more on this). And when I say important I mean imperative. The incoming leader should be able to directly tie security activities highlighted in the agenda to the organisation's strategy, goals, mission, and objectives. Essentially, security has no choice but to move forward based on the commercial drivers of the organisation.[12]

Documenting and delivering a cyber security agenda that is aligned to the business strategy will give the incoming leader a starting point and a foundation on which to build a detailed information security strategy.

When it comes to strategic alignment of the agenda, there are few things to consider:

1. First, what sort of business are you in? A start-up? A long-established iconic brand? What industry are you in and how much change is your organisation going through? (This list is by no means exhaustive.) The answers will help you to understand your risk.

2. What is the business's ultimate goal in its one-year plan? This might be a 50% growth in customers/members, making more profit than your competitors, being number one in the industry, being an employer of choice… The list goes on.

3. Think about how security will add value to the business strategy. What does the organisation care most about?

   a. If it's maintaining the trust of your clients, protecting their data is key.
   b. If it's being the leading edge in research and development, protection of intellectual property and confidentiality will be a focus.
   c. If you are a content provider, you must prioritise integrity and availability of data and services.

With this in mind, take what the business cares most about and convert that into focal points for the security agenda. If the overall business strategy is to move from a traditionally analog organisation to a digital one, you may have developers committing code to public websites or apps. If so, and they are not coding within secure code guidelines, one of your big rocks might be to examine application security. This may also feed the type of leader you select or the type of team they build.

If you are a start-up and experiencing exponential growth, your overall strategic plan may include continuing this trajectory.

However, you might be using some tools and systems that were right-fit to store data when you were 'young'. As you grow, however, this becomes unsustainable. If this data is sensitive or contains private information, a key priority for your new leader will be to advise on security practices to protect that information, both on behalf of the customer and also in line with privacy laws. In this case, one of the big rocks becomes data security/protection.

As a bonus, getting this alignment right will inform your communications plan, because your security messaging isn't only about having a secure password and not clicking on links. It's about security's role in taking the business forward.

Key takeaway

The agenda is not a strategy. It's a starting point in considering how security can add value to what your business is focused on achieving in the next 12 months, outside of business as usual, of course.

Section 2

Compass: What's your destination?

'The secret of change is to focus all of your energy, not on fighting the old but on building the new.'

Socrates

Part 2 of the framework is Compass, which is about understanding where you are going, based on your agenda. Also, what skills does your organisation need, based on the overall business strategy?

When we plan, we often overestimate what we can achieve and underestimate the resources needed to achieve it. This is true for most aspects of work and life, and is certainly true for security.

Whether you hire a sole security professional or team will dictate the workload and variety of tasks the individual(s) can take on and the level of involvement they need to have in certain activities. As this book is focused on hiring leaders, my advice would be to focus your efforts on fundamental, measurable areas for security improvement that are aligned with your organisation's priorities and key risks. This will ensure your initiatives relate to what's really important, and make security part of the achievement of your organisation's overall strategy. Be honest about the change your organisation is capable of achieving, and what it will take to achieve it, and you're much more likely to hire a security leader who can execute a strong, visible program in the coming year.

6

Where to?

'A goal properly set is halfway reached.'

Zig Ziglar, *author*

The next two or three chapters work hand in hand. What you are looking to achieve by hiring a cyber or information security professional is closely linked with what skills and attributes you feel are non-negotiable in a successful candidate, and therefore what comprises a realistic job description.

Thinking about what you want to achieve is important when it comes to 'selling' the job to a potential candidate. Being honest about their role, why they will be in the organisation, how they will be supported, and the perception of the security function are essential in choosing the right candidate.

I have worked in many organisations, some with extensive security funding, some without. Some where the role of the security leader was a carefully considered addition to a team and others where the security leader occupied the only security role.

Often, when a position is newly created, it has come about because of a large-scale breach/incident – not always debilitating, but big enough to rattle the organisation into action – an audit committee finding, a direction from a nervous board, or the instinct of a CEO/CIO/CTO that a security leader is needed. If it is a replacement of an existing leader, there will usually be a discussion about re-justifying the role's existence and whether there is a way for existing staff to absorb the role. Ideally, absorbing the role will not be possible, as the leader plays a significantly different role to a technical engineer, analyst, or adviser.

Through the review of countless job ads and job descriptions, and via conversations at security events, it's become apparent to me that four major outcomes are sought from hiring a security leader. They are not all pretty.

To satisfy an audit finding

If you are hiring a head of cyber or information security only because an audit report advised you to, they will never be able to achieve anything more than the perception of good security. They could become a figurehead who makes it look like the business is protecting itself and the customer, when it is not.

Creating the agenda and finding out how the rest of the executive team and stakeholders feel about security goes a long way to starting a broader conversation about security and gaining better traction for the new leader. By all means, use the audit committee direction as leverage, but it can't be the only rationale. As CIO, you need to buy into the benefits of what this leader can achieve, and why a dedicated expert should be armed with the resources (time and people) to provide more than audit remediation. I'm aware that audit remediation goes a long way to securing an organisation. But if the leader spends all their time looking back, they will never have the capacity to plan, to future-proof the organisation, and look forward.

Fulfilling security needs with one person

If you are hiring a security leader to address *all* the security concerns in the organisation, they will also be doomed to fail (or depart). This is yet another reason to consider the big rocks: What is the priority and where do you want to focus first? This new leader is likely to need a team at some stage, or at least a community of practice, where those who do not report to the head of information security but have a security-related function can come together to ensure they share the same objective.

Compliance

A number of regulations and laws require that particular organisations have a dedicated information or cyber security head, someone identified as the officer responsible for security. Hiring for compliance usually takes the form of nominating an internal staff member. This person won't necessarily have the skills, knowledge, or care factor to address risk or incidents, but their name will appear on documentation, and any audit against compliance will be met.

Certainty and confidence

Overwhelmingly, the most common response can be summarised similar to this one, from a CIO in Australia when asked why they would hire a security leader: 'It means there is a dedicated, subject-knowledgeable person whose sole role is to mitigate the organisation's security risks'.

During my research on the objective of hiring a security leader, some CIOs gave the responses below. Can you relate to any of these?

- Having a security leader provides organisational focus and prioritisation of security.
- It ensures we have someone who is defining a clear strategy and directing traffic when it comes to our overall approach to managing and executing our cyber security activities.
- Without a leader, the danger is that we don't take an holistic approach, and our investment is over- or under-balanced due to individual department priorities or preferences.
- We need a competent champion whose sole focus is ensuring that cyber security is taken seriously and that we are investing appropriately in the areas that matter most.

- The executive team looks to the cyber security leader to define the information security program and its subsequent management, and provide education and guidance to all.
- As CIO, cyber security is one of my two greatest concerns. (The other is talent). Without a cyber person, the front door doesn't feel locked, and the business is more reactive to security issues.
- We need this person for compliance, someone with deep security knowledge and whose daily task is to focus on cyber security – to prevent attacks, respond to incidents, speak to audit and risk, and give the board confidence that cyber is being handled.
- The current IT security manager is focused on policy and compliance, and without a more senior leader, security will remain a desk function.

Key takeaway

No matter your destination, make sure it's well thought through, respectful of the security talent you engage, and is based on an agenda that key stakeholders can and will support.

7

What skills and outcomes are non-negotiable?

To pick up a point from chapter 5, it is often the case that a new security leader is given the responsibility of many. This may be because the organisation hasn't had someone addressing cyber risk before. This leads to a lack of understanding of what one person can achieve, so they are given too broad a remit. It may also be because funding accommodates only one security staff member, and a leader is chosen as the best investment. Finally, it may be that a team is planned, but for now, the security leader has all the responsibility.

These are quite valid reasons for heaping tasks and outcomes on the new leader. However, this is not sensible or reasonable, and a laundry list of responsibilities can turn away great candidates. (More on this in chapter 8).

To combat this at a time when your long-term strategy and team are still a way off, it is important to be comfortable with what is and isn't negotiable when you meet candidates. This means establishing what skills and abilities are needed on day one. Keep this squarely in your mind as you assess your non-negotiables.

Much of this will be considered when agreeing on content for the job description. Here are some examples of non-negotiable skills/experience that my clients have asked for:

- The candidate must have led/delivered a security strategy before.
- The candidate must previously have worked as a head of information security

- The candidate's experience cannot solely be from [insert particular industry]. (This is often requested if the hiring manager doesn't want someone whose whole career has been with the big four, for example.)
- The candidate must have delivered outcomes/content to boards (be 'board-ready').
- The candidate must have previously led cyber security incident response activities.

Non-negotiables can also take the form of attributes or qualities such as:

- resilience
- curiosity
- patience
- empathy
- adaptability
- ability to influence

Non-negotiables are key to the hiring process, yet they can be overlooked because a candidate seems so great that you are willing to negotiate the non-negotiable, or you choose based on hiring fatigue. This is the last thing you should do. You also need to be willing to test these, both in reviewing the résumés and in interviewing candidates. Ask candidates to share examples of when they exhibited each attribute. You will also want to test this with referees when you get to that point in the process.

And what about nice-to-haves? That second tier of desires that are negotiable but would be nice to have for cultural or role-based reasons? Things such as:

1. *A female.* (Females are becoming more sought after for several reasons: Women tend to take a different approach to their roles/teams/jobs; are needed in the security industry; are seen to fulfil diversity needs; and, as their numbers grow,

can begin to change a patriarchal culture, if that's the impact you seek.) A mere 11% of cyber security professionals are women,[13] allegedly because their higher education tends to be in non-technical areas, lack of awareness of the jobs available, discrimination, and slow social advancement. Women, of course, should be hired because they are the right person for the role, not merely because of their gender. But due to these reasons detailed by global research, fewer women are attracted to the industry.

2. *Certifications.* While it has been argued that certain security certifications help to ensure that the industry is speaking the same 'language', these certifications do not necessarily mean the candidate is a competent security operator. These certifications are nice to have but should not discount a candidate if they otherwise meet all your non-negotiables. (This is also why I put certification in the nice-to-have section, because if they are non-negotiable, you can miss out on some good candidates who haven't seen a need, or had a desire, to certify. More on this in chapter 8.)

A few things to note:

- Non-negotiables, especially when it comes to traits, should be in line with your company values (expectations) and with what it's truly like to work in your organisation (reality).
- If you are the one setting the non-negotiables, don't be too quick to delegate the early interview process. Non-negotiables should be addressed/tested in the first interview to avoid wasting your and the candidate's time.
- When you interview, after the initial chatter, let the candidate speak first. If you launch into the role, and the company, and all the reasons you're hiring, you're writing the script for them. Since they don't know what you want to hear, you are more likely to get an authentic retelling of their history, including

successes and failures, than if you had led the conversation with role requirements.

If you are a CIO reading this, it is not my objective to tell you how to sweep up. I realise that by this time in your career, chances are you have interviewed and hired many staff. The point of this chapter is that security leaders, and all security professionals, cannot fulfil the role of many, and yet often they are required to do this, even for a short period.

So, if you design what you absolutely need from day one in skills and experience and let other, less pressing tasks/skills go, you will have more success in hiring sooner rather than later. Remember, though, to also set/assure the expectations of others involved – especially when the role is new and everyone has a view on what the leader should be capable of. (More on this in chapters 11 and 13.)

Key takeaway

There is no right or wrong. While I may or may not agree with your non-negotiables, you are setting them, you have to work with this person every day, and you see these as imperatives. Remember that the more non-negotiables you have, the narrower your market becomes. Non-negotiables ensure that you seek a candidate who can, at a minimum, meet the security needs of your organisation in the short to medium term.

Bonus material

While you are the one who needs to establish your list of needs and non-negotiables, this blog post I wrote in 2016 about the qualities security leaders need may help in your ponderings.

Top 7 qualities of an Information Security Leader

In the security industry, like any other, there are a few traits that should be on your list of non-negotiables when it comes to hiring a leader. The information security leader is one of the key roles in business today and is not a hire that you can afford to get wrong. Here are the top 7 qualities to look for, in no particular order (except the first one):

1. *Integrity.* This needs little explaining in a candidate for an information security leadership role. Integrity is without question the key attribute to seek. The bonus is honest, ethical, loyal, consistent and responsible are all values that can come with high integrity leaders.

2. *Competence.* A candidate's competence can be established in their demonstrated prioritisation, innovation, delivery, ability to get the job done, exceeding expectations and evidenced uplift of an organisation. In addition to this, their desire to increase their level of competence through on-the-job skills and training must be continuous.

3. *Leadership.* It may seem strange to call out leadership as a skill that a leader needs, but beyond people leadership, information security leaders need to be able to demonstrate taking charge, problem solving and inspiring teams and boards to make change and embrace new ways of working. Not all leaders are created equal and someone who has led before isn't automatically the right leader for your organisation.

4. *Connections/networks.* Networking is a skill that not only helps in connecting to the security community, it shows willingness to engage peers and stakeholders in new conversations. Networking promotes the leader and your business, connects the organisation with other brilliant talent and highlights potential partnerships.

5. *Technical know-how.* Gone are the days of professionals suggesting that they are 'not technical' (I was once guilty of

this). In this digital economy, every business leader including those in security must have the know-how to speak to technical staff in the organisation to understand and achieve the organisational strategy. This doesn't mean finding a leader who can code with your best developers. But it does mean they understand how technology impacts the broader business objectives.

6. *Resilience*. Embodying the above traits every day can be exhausting for many – but there are certainly candidates out there that take this in their stride. Leading a security team or function requires the ability to react quickly and wisely to security events and rapid business growth. This, like integrity, will need to be established early in the hiring process.

7. *Gravitas*. Security has been known to be a dry, compliance-driven topic (hard to believe, I know). Candidates with gravitas deliver information with just the right amount of seriousness and commitment to command respect. Gravitas is not only important when addressing senior leaders and the board, but is key in delivering advice during projects, negotiating with third parties and in incident response.

A great information security leader will be vital in times of disaster, during business growth and in day-to-day operations. Hiring based on the above qualities will stand you in good stead for the breadth of outcomes they may be charged to deliver. Are you looking for these attributes in your next information security leader?

8

Let's get real – the true job description

'If NASA was focusing on looking for skilled moon walkers, we never would have found people to go to the moon.'

Anonymous

Have you ever read through a job description and wondered what is it they really want? Job descriptions (JDs) are notoriously broad. In some ways, this is needed to cover the spectrum of what might come across a person's desk on any given day, right? But a JD that's too broad can do a number of things:

1. Turn away candidates who can't fulfil every item on the list

2. Deter candidates who don't want to execute every/any item on the list

3. Discourage candidates who feel that any job description that broad must not be well thought through

4. Invite candidates who can do one of the items on the list and plan to wing the other 49

5. Dissuade qualified candidates, because it's not clear what the key responsibilities are

It may seem that bringing in more candidates is a positive thing. But, in reality, it creates time-sucking résumé review and doesn't benefit anyone. JDs are not the place to build in stretch targets. And yet, security JDs are some of the stretchiest I have seen.

The following list of skills/experience is taken from an actual security job description for a single role:

- Must have prior experience building a security operations centre
- Responsible for strategic direction of information security within the organisation across two countries
- Responsible for ensuring compliance with internal and external information security requirements and standards, e.g., information security policy, ISO27001 principles, and relevant accreditation requirements, e.g., IRAP
- Policy and framework development
- Program administration and delivery
- Compliance
- Incident response activities
- Client surveillance audits
- Due diligence questionnaires /RFPs
- Strong operational security background
- Strong program management – ideally within a vendor or consulting environment
- Experience in environments which require strong internal stakeholder management

There is no mention of a team in the JD so the candidates reading this would assume this is autonomous, and that most of this work would be carried out by them. A JD seeking staff who have run a security operations centre, had strategic experience, worked within a vendor or big four, written policies and responded to RFPs (requests for proposal), and ensured compliance to international standards –

will this really all be required within the next two years? Or is the priority the security operations centre, with a view to grooming this leader to become a strategic player?

> **Side note:** Coaching and mentorship to groom for leadership are greatly needed in the security industry. Recent surveys globally show that professionals are crying out for opportunities which offer professional growth.

When thinking about JDs, consider the shorter term and be realistic. Get some advice on writing a great JD if you're unsure, so you know you will appeal to the type of security leader you need.

A word about women

As mentioned at the start of this chapter, in 2017, about 11% of people in cyber security roles are women,[14] depending on which study you read. There is strong concern within the industry – and backed by the research below – that this stems from women believing they cannot achieve all the items in a job ad, so they don't apply.

> 'According to reports, including the commonly cited internal Hewlett-Packard study, the women working at HP only applied for promotions when they met 100% of the qualifications listed in the job posting, as opposed to men, who would apply if they met 60%. It's been deduced that the lack of women in upper management was due to a lack of confidence among women. However, a [more] recent study was conducted based on the findings at HP, and outlined in an article for Harvard Business Review: *digging deeper into the confidence gap phenomenon. Over a thousand professional men and women were surveyed and asked, "If you decided not to apply for a job because you didn't meet all the qualifications, why didn't you apply?"*

'According to the findings, confidence or lack thereof, was actually the least common reason men and women did not apply. Instead, the most common response, with 46.4% of men and 40.6% of women choosing it as their first reason, was: "I didn't think they would hire me since I didn't meet the qualifications and I didn't want to waste my time and energy". Survey responders didn't lack confidence in their ability or their skills, instead they were interpreting the job description as a hard and fast outline of skills and experience a qualified candidate must have".'[15]

Megan Noel

If we want to expand the industry, we need to do a few things. First, get real about the JD and what is truly needed in the first instance. Second, stop using advertising as the only mechanism to recruit, and get out to networking events and meet the men and women you require. Finally, realise that security staff come from diverse backgrounds and many have had some very specialised experience. We need to allow them to evolve into a role, to invest in their professional development and allow room for stretch (more on that in chapter 12). I'm not suggesting we put the organisation at risk by employing underqualified candidates who can't provide the minimum viable outcomes needed for the role just because they are women, or just because they are men. I'm suggesting that new ways of attracting and retaining security professionals are needed, and JDs play a part in this.

For a realistic job description, stick to the requirements/ expectations you have of this person for the next 12–18 months. The security person you need today is not the security person you need in two years' time. Security evolves, and it evolves quickly. Today, you might need someone who has great start-up skills – vendor management, application security, thought leadership, and innovative ideas to create a secure culture. In two years' time, you might need to 'calm the farm', as they say, and consider compliance, identity management, or security in acquisitions.

When I asked CIOs if the security posture made a difference to whom they hired, the responses were mixed. Yes; no; maybe; not really. But you can't carry the same detailed job description across many years and hope that the security function will continue to grow and prosper. JDs are living documents, and you can still adjust for change and growth without taking away from the core accountability of the role.

Aside from your near-term focus, here are some tips to assemble a more realistic job description:

- Be careful about what is desired, mandatory, and 'an advantage'. Think carefully about what you put under each of these headlines. Does your security leader really need every certification? Do they need a background in financial services just because you are a bank? Is strategic planning really just desired? I'm not suggesting any of these are wrong, or right, but be clear on your mandatory expectations and non-negotiables, and be even clearer on what you could sacrifice in return for a candidate who is 75% there.
- This document is needed for performance reviews and against which you will manage your new leader. You can't afford for it to be too subjective.
- Set realistic expectations for workloads and responsibilities.
- Be clear about how the role fits in with the rest of the organisation.
- Be clear about the short- and longer-term goals.
- Provide a definition of success. Any JD that's too broad can appear insurmountable for a candidate or employee, and success can seem a distant oasis.
- Strike a balance between brevity and detail. More than two or three pages and you're likely to lose the reader on a number of levels.

Certifications, boom or bust?

Security certifications, such as CISSP/CISM/CISA/CEH, are fast becoming the norm in job descriptions as a measurable way to assess a candidate's expertise and as a screening mechanism for human resources. However, the value of security certifications has long been debated. There are many schools of thought on requiring certifications in job descriptions. Here are a few that have been expressed to me over the years:

1. Certifications are a must-have, especially when hiring 'technical' security staff, as people who come together who have the same certifications are able to speak a common language on security.

2. CISSP, for example, is not easy, at 250 questions and up to six hours, to sit. But it is argued that all a security certification proves is that you can successfully read a book, sit an exam, and pay a huge fee, as all the content is available to be studied from a textbook. The bottom line is it provides theory, but not on-the-job training.

3. Certifications are of value if you are early in your career, or are new to information security after years in another profession; however, given the prerequisite years of experience required in order to qualify, it's out of reach for those who need it most.

4. Certifications that are outdated in terms of the technology they teach, platforms they rely on, or policies to live by are useless, but an assessing CIO or hiring manager may not be aware of this.

5. Certifications that are software-specific, such as Microsoft, Cisco, and Oracle, are considered of more value than a security-specific qualification.

6. A security leader with an MBA is of far greater value than someone who has put in the same hours studying for CISSP or similar.

7. Leadership experience, networking, and attending relevant industry meetings/conferences is, collectively, of greater value than a certification gained five years before.

8. Certifications can provide base-level confidence to CIOs who are unable to confidently assess security candidates. Achieving a certification also shows that they have some commitment to continued learning in the security industry.

9. Many different certifications are available. Ultimately, the application of the candidate's knowledge is more important than the number of certifications someone has achieved.

10. Completing too many certifications can suggest a lack of career focus and planning. Certifications should support your career direction rather than be achieved to meet a job description for leadership roles.

There is always the option to hire someone whom you believe can meet your non-negotiables and some of your less urgent requirements. Once on board, offer to put them through certification if it means a lot to you as a leader/line manager, or to align the candidate with their security peers in the organisation. Investing in staff can provide not only upskilling of your team but increase the likelihood of retention and job satisfaction. Some certifications are not cheap, from both a financial and time commitment. Offering your team a chance to increase their skills and knowledge while they are in a role can do wonders for morale and commitment.

Side note: Some items that might be of equal or greater value than certifications when hiring include joining professional institutions/organisations dedicated to security (ISACA, OWASP, Cloud Security Alliance, Australian Information Security Association, or your local equivalent), keynote speaking, and volunteering with security associations.

A word on job titles

There is a plethora of job titles that are often – and in a well-intentioned way – used interchangeably. But a head of security is not the same as a head of cyber security or a head of information security, which is not the same as an IT security manager, which can't be interchanged with a chief information security officer. By all means make the job title enticing, but not so much so that people aren't sure they would want to take it on, or that it can't be found when a job search is performed. You may also need to test the market, and if traditional job titles aren't drawing in the candidates you are after, consider changing the title but ensure it still reflects the level and breadth of responsibility.

Also, consider the type of candidate who would be attracted to particular titles. I, for example, would not feel confident applying for a role with the word 'engineer' in the title. I saw an ad for what appeared to be a head of information security role that used the word engineer in the title to attract more candidates. There are those who have had chief information security officer titles but would not apply for a manager role, and those who may not realise the seniority of a position titled CISO (because the role reports to the CIO).

Some questions to ask yourself:

- What will this leader need to achieve in the next 12–18 months?
- What job title clearly describes the responsibilities and level of authority/hierarchy of this role?
- Do I need candidates to possess certifications, and are these truly needed to measure candidates against one another?

- How can I attract more female candidates to ensure I have a varied candidate pool?

Key takeaway

The job description wears many hats. Not only does it detail success factors, it's a great trigger for valuable, relevant interview questions. It's also a commitment by the business to support the activities laid out in it, so socialise it with your c-level peers before finalising it, and be careful what you wish for. Remember to consider the role title and function when pulling the JD together, and how the required experience can play a significant role in who applies. It may be that your HR department has to create a new category for security role titles if they don't fit a mould.

Section 3

Connection: How to hire?

'Hiring the best is your most important task.'

Steve Jobs, *co-founder, Apple Inc.*

No part of the framework is more important than another. The work you have put in so far to understand what's important to you and the organisation and what you won't budge on will hold you in good stead for the guts of the hiring process. Meeting a lot of candidates can be disheartening and also frustrating when you have a clear vision of what you want. It can also be uplifting and inspiring as you see the potential in each one. As I said in Part 2, have some non-negotiables and also some room to move if the cultural fit is going to far outweigh anything you can teach or have the leader coached in. Obviously, experience is required to get the job done. But consider the great opportunity for your talented employee should you find room for growth.

Part 3 of the framework is all about connection with the right candidates. Finding and retaining cyber security professionals starts with deciding how you will source the candidates –yourself, via a recruiter or using an internal talent team. From initial search to interview and ultimately offering someone the role. Connecting with the right people is key. The components of connection are: assessing the candidates for their fit, technical and cultural, having the right co-interviewer, and realising you might get away with hiring the person you know in your gut is right, even though the role will be a stretch for them. This is a tough process and one you can't afford to get wrong.

9

To recruiter or not to recruiter?

'Time spent on hiring is time well spent.'

Robert Half, *pioneer recruiter*

On any given day, on LinkedIn, you can read blunt, jaded posts about a 'potential candidate' being approached by a recruiter for roles they could never do. Or roles they did 10 years ago. Or they've been approached because they are a woman (or because they are not).

Since leaving my corporate job and beginning my business in 2016, I have been approached at least five times in 12 months by recruiters who say, 'We were just wondering where your new business was at, because we have this great role. We know you're doing consulting now, but you might still be interested in a permanent job instead.' The frustrating part about this is that for some of the jobs I'm not qualified, or I'm over-qualified, but because I have a passion for security, they seem to think their role is the one that will make me leave my consulting business to return to the fold. I politely decline, but I'm sure they are hanging up just to call the next person who fits the title they are seeking to fill. I'm generalising to the recruiters I have been exposed to of late, but this simply does not fill me with confidence when it comes to recruiters finding candidates for security leadership roles.

Many recruiters are the first to admit they don't know how to fill these roles. Security roles are new to human resource people and recruiters. Their eyes glaze over when security staff talk technical. They don't understand that one security leader may have completely different skills to another, yet they have the same title, pay grade, and years in the industry. It's totally possible that one CISO could not simply walk into the job of another.

There are many great recruiters out there who have security roles to fill because they are on a panel with an employer and are contracted to fill any position that employer requires. This can be frustrating to recruiters who specialise in security because they can't provide their expertise to these organisations as they are not part of the panel process. Furthermore, if a panel recruiter cannot fill the role, the CIO often independently heads out to market, which is usually just as problematic if they haven't first had the hard conversations and put in the groundwork recommended in this book.

There is significant value in your legwork, preparing for what the future security of the organisation will look like and therefore what type of leader you need. If you can do this preparation and conduct the recruitment in house with your HR team to support you, this is a good option. However, if you are considering using third-party recruiters, there are some key things to keep in mind.

- Look for a recruiter who is aware the state of the security market. They can give a realistic view about your potential for hiring sooner rather than later.
- Target a recruiter who attends security events and understands the security challenges facing organisations.
- Find a recruiter you enjoy speaking to. You need open dialogue and trust to find a stellar candidate. This comes only with being open to honest conversations and not cringing when the phone rings. Recruiters are sales people, so their ways will be different to yours, but building a strong relationship is of great value.

General cons to using a recruiter:

- They are not you (of course). You know in your mind exactly what you want, because you have done the hard thinking, planning, and legwork, so handing that over to someone else will always come with risks.
- You (or someone you trust) still needs to spend time interviewing and meeting candidates. This is costing your or your employee's productivity, which would have been used anyway, without the third-party recruiter. Every hour you spend reading CVs and interviewing adds to the cost of recruitment, because if you place one of their people, you pay the recruiter for that privilege.
- There are very few true security recruiters who are passionate about the subject and the professionals involved, which may lead to shortlists of people who are not your ideal candidate.
- They can't measure culture. They are not working in the environment every day to know exactly the type of candidate that will 'fly' within your organisation. This means potentially meeting more candidates than you had planned. (As a side note, this could also be a pro, as the more you meet, the better feel you will get for the security skills that fit best.)

If you have to use one, I recommend finding security-specific recruiters who can deal directly with you or with your human resource consultants. This isn't always possible, so, if you are planning – or forced by company policy – to use a panel recruitment company, go back and read section 2 again to be clear on your job description and objectives. This will help you to be doubly clear on what you want to achieve in the next one to two years, what experience or skills are negotiable, and ensure you have a clear job description. These steps will lead to a clearer job ad and more useful conversations with other potential candidates whom you might meet at networking events or through your contacts. (More on that in chapter 11.)

Resources:
Here are a few dedicated cyber security recruiters in Australia:

- CyberSecPeople   https://www.cybersecpeople.com
- Decipher Bureau   https://www.decipherbureau.com
- Q1 Recruitment   https://q1group.com.au

Key takeaway

If you must use a recruiter, try to find a skilled cyber security recruiter. Do your homework and plan for the process with a clear direction and job description. See section 2 for more information.

10

Candidate review

*'I would rather interview 50 people and
not hire anyone than hire the wrong person.'*

Jeff Bezos, *CEO of Amazon*

This book is not here to tell you how to do your job. If you have been successfully recruiting IT leaders and professionals for years, you might think this chapter won't have value for you, but I encourage you to read it anyway.

Early in my career, my employer sent me on a course called Network Engineering for Non-network Engineers. As you might imagine from its catchy title, the course explained a complex communications network to those like me who were responsible for talking about it to the public. Recalling this course years later reminds me that even somewhat alien subject matter can be valuable to those from another area of business or industry. This is also true when it comes to some of the amazing 'security people' I have met through my career. I am using quote marks because, in many cases, calling them security people isn't a complete truth.

Many admired security leaders are appointed, asked, or 'voluntold' into security roles based on anything but their technical security skills, and via some pretty unusual paths. Despite lacking hands-on security experience, these souls were chosen for qualities that can't be trained, such as their integrity, their inherent leadership skills, and their clear understanding of right from wrong. Many security people are also chosen because they are great communicators, team builders, or can rally the troops when hard times hit. History has shown that filling security roles with unlikely candidates has brought into the industry cross-functional role models with an understanding of business-related risk – experience that some lifelong security professionals never acquire.

My point is that when considering security leaders, chances are the CVs you see will come from varied backgrounds. I know well-respected security leaders who cut their teeth in HR, audit, the police force, armed services, risk, technology, PR, or academia. Their more recent experience is what you are most focused on, given the pace of security these days, but consider their background as a bonus in terms of your agenda. Some leaders bring unique skills and experience, and should not be discounted because they did not take a traditional computer science path.

This can also be important in reviewing candidates, because you may not see all the CVs that come in. Depending on how you recruit, another person tasked with CV review may be screening out 'unsuitable' applicants. This may be a recruiter, a human resources manager, one of your direct reports, another security staff member, or a third-party consultant who vets the CVs for you.

The vetting process is also something to consider. If you have created a great job description, have briefed the reviewer on your priorities, and trust their judgement, you're halfway there. This process will certainly save you time if you find the shortlist hits the mark. If the CVs you see look like the best of a bad bunch, it might be worth doing some spot-checking or taking a deeper look at the rejection list. This quality assurance could make or break your recruitment process. However, your preparation and trust in the process should yield a good shortlist.

Alternatively, you may receive no shortlist at all. This is not necessarily a bad thing if none of the candidates come close to meeting your non-negotiables. However, I would be surprised if you found no one worth interviewing, because people on paper are often very different face to face. Trusting only a CV could mean missing out on a good candidate who hasn't sold their skills the way you expect.

A note on CVs

The CV is a window into what the candidate sees as important and can help with job and cultural fits. My CV leads with how I have positively influenced people through my career. This has always been my priority. Others might lead with accolades, certifications, companies they have represented, or technical achievements. There is no right or wrong, but a CV is much more than a historical document. As a hiring manager, look into how it is put together and the vibe you get from the candidate's approach to their past and future. It's quite two-dimensional, and sometimes you need to trust your gut. Given that how the candidate represents themselves is probably how they would represent you and your organisation, after your initial 30-second judgement, here are some things to look out for.

1. **Spelling errors and poor wording**. If you expect the successful candidate to express themselves well in written and verbal communications and their CV is poorly worded, this should be of concern. This document shows their ability to talk about a subject they know well, so it should be well put together, succinct, and clear.

2. **Vague.** Look carefully at the way information about achievements is presented. If all the responsibilities or achievements focus on what a group, team, or organisation achieved, with no detail about the individual's contribution, how will you know their strengths?

3. **Initiative.** Look for the outcomes/achievements gained that they weren't paid to do, such as exceeding a target rather than just meeting it, or receiving a special commendation.

Next stop – meeting the candidates. After the CVs are reviewed, chatting to a candidate face to face is the time to consider fit.

Their approach to you, the language they use, and their general demeanour speak volumes about how they will fit into the role. As a female, I often find the approach of a male industry peer is to take on different guises, from approachable and respectful to threatening or arrogant. I'm sure this is also true in reverse. Also, consider if the interviewee responds to your basic questions with a lot of technical language. This is concerning as you are their target audience in day-to-day activities, and their delivery to you should be pitched appropriately, which, as a good leader, they should be able to judge.

Consider that the new security leader will need to be passionate, driven, and influential. No matter the maturity of the organisation, these traits are a given to be tested. I have interviewed candidates who are perfect on paper, but when I met them, they were jaded and had lost their drive to change the world one phishing link at a time, so to speak. Think back to your non-negotiables and ensure that your questions are focused on both the hard skills and personal traits you are keen to confirm are present.

This process of candidate review can also be influenced by a detail I discuss in the next chapter. Your approach (and theirs) might be slightly different if you have met the candidate before, or they are known to someone in your organisation.

If you do find yourself without good prospective candidates at this stage, I recommend you revisit your job description, reassess your non-negotiables, and reconsider your method for attracting candidates, i.e., if online ads aren't working, try more networking, or vice versa, or reconsider the job title.

Key takeaway

Candidate review is challenging, and you can easily grow disheartened. Push on with your screening and face-to-face interviews. Revisit your method of attracting candidates and your interview questions if you find you cannot glean the information you need to assess the candidate properly.

11

Surround yourself with supporters

'You need to have a collaborative hiring process.'

Steve Jobs, *co-founder, Apple Inc.*

There are times in the hiring process when you will need to surround yourself with certain people, professionals and peers. This will ensure that you make the best attempt at finding the right person. Furthermore, trying to do the hiring alone is futile. You might find support of value at the following stages: when seeking referrals from employees, when seeking candidates, and when selecting those to co-interview with you.

Internal employee referrals

One of the best ways to find and retain great talent, security or otherwise, is via referral. Providing a brief job description to staff/ employees to see if they know anyone who might have the suitable skills and cultural fit is a great place to start. Your employees are a walking advertisement. Most people wouldn't recommend their friends/acquaintances to work in an organisation they aren't happy to promote, so, in theory, you will only hear from those who are living the values. Furthermore, referrals can be paid/rewarded/ recognised to incentivise staff. While budget can be a concern, even when referrals are paid for, the fee far undercuts anything you would pay a recruiter for the same outcome. A well-designed employee referral program with clear rules and guidelines can deliver candidates straight to your door.

> **Note:** While I never want to suggest things can go sour, it is important to ensure the rules are clear and that you have thought this through. If in doubt, seek legal advice to ensure you cover all potential outcomes should the referred employee not work out.

The process of seeking a referral can also be a great opportunity to promote security within your organisation. Current employees can understand more about what this role will involve and therefore become more aware of the changes a security leader will bring.

The key benefits of a referred candidate are:

1. **Quality**: Studies in the U.S. by employee success software firm Achievers has shown that referred employees are higher-quality recruits. This is because employees pre-screen potential candidates for skills and cultural fit before referring them for a role.

2. **Cost**: Referral programs keep recruitment costs down. They will cost a few thousand dollars now and then, compared with tens of thousands for recruiters. This small army of worker bees out in the community helping your search efforts cannot be underestimated.

3. **Brand**: Referrals are great for your brand as it gets people talking about you, especially on social media such as LinkedIn or Twitter. The message is positive, and even if it doesn't provide a fruitful referral, it will promote your company and its security efforts. Furthermore, employees generally take a

less aggressive approach than recruiters, so their promotion of a job may be better received by their connections.

4. **Morale**: Your people are your ambassadors, and having them understand the goals and direction of the organisation in order to brief a potential candidate only strengthens their passion for the organisation.

Networking

When seeking candidates, networking is close to employee referrals as a winning formula. It is estimated that 85-plus per cent of people who land open jobs did so through networking.[16] Networking with peer CIOs, attending security-related events and speaking at events where security staff – or future security leaders – gather increases your chances of sourcing great talent. Surrounding yourself with other CIOs who have been through a similar process can be helpful. Hearing their war stories, their successes, and how they have managed security can provide insight into what others experience, and you can also learn from their good or bad fortune. They may also have candidates who weren't suitable for their roles but could be for yours. Furthermore, networking directly with those who might be interested in working with/for you is a great approach. There are conferences, meet-ups, informal breakfasts, awards dinners, large events, and drinks you can join to meet more security professionals and, just as importantly, hear about the challenges they face. Two birds, one stone.

Networking is not everyone's cup of tea. Some people simply don't like people. (Strange, but true!) Without networking, I would not have known about any of the jobs I have held since leaving university – and I wouldn't have some of my great friends either! Every one of my jobs has been suggested to me through people I have known or those I have made it my business to know.

The old adage 'It's not what you know, it's who you know' became an old adage thanks to networking. I implore you, next time you get the opportunity, to make the effort to network. Accept an invite to lunch, strike up a conversation, or find an informal activity you can attend where you might meet someone who knows someone who is interested in the role you have on offer.

As a side note, it might be worth contacting some security-focused associations to understand the networking opportunities they have, or to advertise your role with their members if they are up for that. If you're in Australia, the Australian Information Security Association and the Australian Women in Security Network are two good places to start.

The right people to co-interview

Last, but by no means least, choose the right people to co-interview your candidate. At all stages of recruitment, the people you surround yourself with are key to selecting the candidate that fits. This can be challenging to get right because it's hard to know how people will react in an interview situation. Some will have preconceived ideas about what is needed in a security professional and others won't have any idea. Either way, considering who is best to share the first, second, and third interview stages is important. Choosing someone who will have a close collaboration with the new leader can be helpful for personality or cultural fit. However, you won't be able to please everyone, so be careful and honest about what you need from that other opinion. The people you select have to buy in to your agenda, your immediate focus, and your non-negotiables if you are to find the most suitable candidate.

A few things to consider about your co-interviewer(s):

- How much will this new employee affect each co-interviewer's daily life?
- Do they know your goals for the new employee, and do they respect them?
- What is your working relationship with them?

- What will the new security leader's working relationship be with the co-interviewers?
- Will you keep the co-interviewer consistent across all interviews or mix up who comes along with you?
- If security is new to your organisation, how well equipped are your co-interviewers to comprehend the candidate's experience?
- Consider gender balance with your co-interviewers

Key takeaway

Consider carefully how to surround yourself with the relevant people to achieve the best outcome. All of the above takes time and effort but can be rewarding if you can find the right candidate based on a referral, a connection with the candidate, and a good interview team.

12

Are you allowing for stretch?

'If your actions inspire others to dream more, learn more, do more, and become more, you are a leader.'

John Quincy Adams, *former US President*

During my time as a manager and a consultant, I have read many excellent CVs and met some brilliant candidates. I've also met some arrogant applicants, some understated leaders, and some unfortunate professionals who are not sure where they are going, or why.

Through a delivery of the framework, I recently met a fantastic candidate – let's call her Jill – whom I later placed and have also coached. I first spotted Jill on an advanced LinkedIn search for talent, way before she was on the radar as an applicant. I reviewed the job description with the hiring manager, readvertised, and the applicants flowed in – more than a hundred. But Jill didn't apply. I looked at her profile again, after little joy with the hundred applicants, but before I got a chance to approach her, she applied. Her background was strong and she had led security teams in some of Australia's biggest brands.

When I met her, I was charmed by her passion, enthusiasm, and down-to-earth approach to security. The talent manager and I recommended Jill for a second interview. She progressed to the third, and then it stalled. As I said in the previous chapter, surrounding yourself with supporters is important. In Jill's case, when the co-interviewer told the hiring manager he wasn't one hundred per cent convinced of her ability to fill the role, progress stopped while they considered the next move. This was partly due to her self-professed nervousness in approaching boards and senior leaders. Jill was strong in other areas and certainly a passionate security leader. She met the other non-negotiables, and while she didn't have the gravitas some other leaders had exhibited, she was a good cultural fit for the organisation.

While they pondered Jill's ability, we presented some other candidates. The field was slim, and given the non-negotiables, even slimmer. I felt Jill could do the job and so I told the hiring manager my story about taking a chance on people. I told him I had moved to Asia and was speaking to regional boards, having never spoken to a board member before. I had made mistakes, but I had good people around me, I made sure I was prepared so as to support my CIO, and I could improve each time.

I also explained that because this was a new role, any new leader would need guidance in navigating the board and the broader business, about what was expected, and how best to impart information to that audience.

This was (and is) a tough role for any new leader to step into. I'm pleased to say the hiring manager chose Jill, and she is still the head of information security (at the time of writing). I've been coaching her through some of her content, strategy, and presentation skills. And because she is aware of the gap in her skills, Jill is working hard to improve these as soon as she can. The way I see it, securing the organisation is her priority, and if the information reaches the appropriate eyes and ears so that timely decisions can be made, then she's fulfilling her role. For now, any improvement in her delivery is a bonus.

I tell this story because while there are many excellent professionals in this field, right-fit security talent is hard to find. And while it's not always appropriate to hire someone who is still maturing, there should be room for stretch, and if you feel the candidate lives the values and can meet most of your wants/needs on day one, consider taking a chance on them. It might just be the opportunity they need and it will be thanks to you. This isn't an easy option and requires work on your part as their manager. But it's something to ponder when considering the protection of your organisation and the opportunity to help someone expand into a well-rounded leader for their next role. Let's face it, while they are making you look good, your job as their boss is to prepare them for the challenges of the future.

> As a side note: If you're not willing or don't have the capacity to support the new leader in closing the gaps in their skills or experience, it's fine to not go down this path. It may cause the role to sit empty for longer, but if you are unable to support a leader growing into the role, it's not fair on any of the parties involved to move forward together.

Key takeaway

I stand by my advice to have some non-negotiables, skills you must have on day one. But if someone has gaps in their experience, consider how you might be the right person to help them overcome these if it wouldn't be detrimental to your goals. Taking a chance on a candidate who is 80% there could be the best thing for all involved. By all means, assess the situation, trust your gut, and, as always, base your decision on the outcomes you want to achieve in the next 12–18 months.

13

What others are saying, Part 2

'When you talk, you are only repeating what you know. But if you listen, you may learn something new.'

14th Dalai Lama, *spiritual leader, Tibetan Buddhism*

By now you will hopefully have met some really talented cyber security leaders. You will have been to some security-related events/meet-ups. You will be surer than ever of your agenda, which of course needs executive endorsement. And you will be preparing to choose a security leader to take through to reference check, contract offer, and ultimate commitment. How does that feel? Great, right?

Or does it feel daunting? Are those around you inquiring about how the hiring is going. And when you tell them you have chosen a candidate, are they questioning your judgement on the skills and experience you view as valuable? Are you concerned that you may not have judged the person's character in terms of business and environmental fit? All of this is normal, and can upset your process, if you let it.

So, what *are* others saying?

Organisational leaders/stakeholders

Some of the reactions of those around you may include:

- surprise, when you discuss the candidate's skills and experience
- concern that the candidate is more junior or senior than expected
- a wish to have some late input into whom you choose if this person will rely heavily on the appointee to deliver certain outcomes or meet audit requirements

The key thing to remember is that, in security, the fact that your organisation will have a dedicated staff member – and perhaps a team – puts you ahead of many other organisations in achieving certainty and protecting your customers. Furthermore, people will always have an opinion on hiring. Bringing in a security leader is a huge step for any organisation, no matter the size, and can only improve security maturity. This new leader will raise the profile of security commitment just by arriving. (More on this in chapter 16.) This is true for new roles and backfills.

The good thing for you is that if you have followed the process in this book – talked to stakeholders, formulated your agenda, and clearly defined the role – you are justified in your selection, which has also been vetted by your co-interviewer(s). I realise there are points along the way where things could have gone amiss. But, essentially, if the person you have chosen meets your non-negotiables and is ready to take on the agenda, in terms of their skill and their passion and your ability and desire to support them, you can rest easier.

The security industry

What others are saying should include the industry. How well connected is this person and do any of your security connections know of them? Are they participating in industry activities, speaking at events, and supporting their peers?

One of my consulting clients pressed the importance of screening candidates who are active members of industry groups. I couldn't agree more with this requirement when it comes to sourcing staff, especially in security. Working in security, you cannot be an island (or under a rock, for that matter). With the landscape changing daily, and all of us feeling our way to some degree, it is imperative that we share with our peers, seek sounding boards, and learn from others' experiences. Let's face it, today's survivor of a cyber-attack is likely to be tomorrow's authority on the topic. The value an audience can take from your experience of securing an organisation is that they might notice something sooner, see the hallmarks of an attack more easily, or simply be able to educate their workforce on new methods of cyber-attack to be aware of.

Is your candidate a sought-after speaker to talk at industry forums and relive incidents or key learnings from their career to date? Whether a long-time member or first-time attendee, if you find candidates who meet your technical requirements *and* show a desire to inspire and be inspired by their peers, these ones are often keepers.

Referees

What others are saying also includes referees. We all know that referees will rarely say bad things about candidates, which is why they are chosen as referees. But questions can be framed in a way to elicit sufficient information about a candidate's abilities and their output without asking for negative comments. Reference checks are sometimes done by HR partners and recruiters, but it is important that you be happy with the depth of the reference check, that it goes beyond the basics. If you have concerns after the checks are done, ask for more referees to delve deeper, or conduct further checking yourself.

Earlier in the book we mentioned testing the candidate's ability to meet non-negotiables through referee questioning. Ask the referee to share examples of times the candidate exhibited some of your non-negotiable experiences or traits.

Some additional questions you might want to ask:

- This role is senior and will involve interacting with the board. How do you think this candidate will manage board expectations?
- How did the candidate manage the stress and impact of security incidents?
- How does the candidate relate to others?
- How did the candidate handle autonomy?
- In terms of budget, did you feel the candidate had a grasp of the best investments for your organisation?

Key takeaway

In life, as a general rule, we should avoid listening to what others think or say and trust our own gut and judgement. This doesn't mean we stop asking questions, seeking opinions, and validating information before we act. Asking some key, open questions, and understanding the value others have gained and continue to gain from your preferred candidate, yields important information for you to consider when selecting your next security leader.

Section 4

Commitment: Are you ready?

'Unless commitment is made, there are only promises and hopes, but no plans.'

Peter F. Drucker, *author*

In 1973, the *Harvard Business Review* ran a story about staff retention: 'Why employees stay'.[17] Almost 45 years later, it still rings true. The premise is that employees stay in organisations because of inertia. Until something better comes along, they will stay in their role. But the push to stop the inertia is affected by four factors.

The first is job satisfaction. Second is the 'company environment' and the degree of comfort an individual employee feels within it.

The article stated, 'An employee's inertia is strengthened or weakened by the degree of compatibility between his own work ethic and the values for which the company stands. The employee's ethic derives from his own values and the actual conditions he encounters on the job. The company's values derive from societal norms, formal decisions by the board of directors, and the policies and procedures of the managing group. A widening gap between these two vantages weakens inertia; a narrowing gap strengthens it.'

The third factor is an employee's perceived job opportunities in other institutions and self-imposed restrictions and personal criteria (such as location). Finally, there are non-work factors such as financial responsibilities, family ties, friendships, and community relations. Many employees in the study reported low job satisfaction, and yet they stayed.

A few years ago I took on a role that provided me with many of the 'personal criteria' I needed. Having just stepped off the plane from three and a half years in Asia, I took a job that gave me much-needed Australian experience. It was a new industry to me, it was a 'head of' position and, most importantly, it gave me flexibility. With two small children and a sick family member, I had returned from Asia to be with them and this job fitted the criteria.

What I didn't realise was that I was joining an organisation that didn't align with my values. And while Harvard might have done this study 45 years ago, all four of these factors came into play when I figured out, only six weeks into the job, that I couldn't work for this organisation.

On reflection, I don't know that I could have perceived this earlier. I was so focused on meeting my family commitments that the organisational match wasn't at the front of my mind enough. I flagged my concerns to a trusted leader, who was not my boss and did a good job of talking me down off the ledge. He was passionate about the organisation and about keeping me in the role, which was flattering and persuasive. I have a lot to thank him for, as he spurred me to look at how I could add value to the organisation, uphold my commitment to the role, and exit with some level of personal integrity, despite the values clash. I took his words with a grateful heart and ploughed on. But within weeks, the shot in the arm he had given me had worn off and I realised, once again, that my heart wasn't in it.

When it comes to retention, there is only so much an organisation can do to keep staff in a role once their inertia has shifted. What is important is making sure you address their needs, discuss the alignment of their values and the support they need to get the job done *before* they sign the employment contract. Make sure they can pass the barbecue test: If they were at a barbecue and someone asked where they worked, would they be proud to say? Make sure the prospective employee realises what they are getting themselves into from a work perspective. (Lucky you have that agenda from chapter 2 handy.) Finally, make sure that the environment in which they will work supports this leader. I'm not asking for special treatment, just due diligence. The security job market is competitive and you want to create the right conditions for your new head of information security or cyber security leader to commit and prosper.

In saying all of this, you must also consider what do *you* need to support them to ensure you can have a long future together in protecting the organisation? You need peer endorsement of the agenda, a budget for the security program, and the support of some of your other direct reports and peers for this recruit. Finally, to obtain the certainty you seek from your security leader, you need to have resilience, to trust in the process, and be ready to commit.

Section 4 of the framework is about committing to the new employee – being comfortable in your selection but also understanding their level of commitment to protecting the organisation and staying with it for the right reasons, not due to inertia.

14

The tour of duty

*'Plan your work for today and every day,
then work your plan.'*

Margaret Thatcher, *former UK Prime Minister*

We all know of people who take on a new role with a plan a mind. They know from day one what their 30-, 60-, and 90-day goals are. Or 'the first 100 days'. There are also planners who consider a limited tenure. I'm generalising, as everyone is slightly different. But, in essence, people either know what they want and how long they plan to allow to achieve it or they go into roles with blind faith that the journey will take them where it takes them.

For those with a plan of big goals and limited tenure, this is often their own boundary to set, but it can work well for the candidate and the organisation. I have a couple of examples.

Example 1:

A friend assumed a role as a consultant leading a team as an interim executive. The business loved her, and before long, they were asking her to stay. She politely declined, every other day for a month, until she went to the chief executive and suggested she would stay, but on the following terms: She would remain a consultant, but only for two years, and in that time she planned to execute X, Y, and Z. With this proposal, the organisation was able to move ahead with consistent leadership, it could plan for the leadership change two years on, and it knew what it would get by agreeing to the deal. It's was a win for both sides.

Example 2:

Some people look for a particular skill set to complement their experience. Early in my career I had a peer who hadn't worked for any smaller companies. He stepped out of a senior role in a global organisation and spent two years to the day leading a much smaller team in a more agile environment – 'agile' in the traditional sense. By his resignation date, he had made himself redundant and moved to a more senior role in a mid-tier organisation – his plan all along. The organisation was aware that he was seeking some specific experience for his CV. They knew he would not stay forever, and because of that, they worked him hard, made sure he trained others, and imparted his 20 years of business knowledge through mentoring and program leadership. The business respected his honesty, and instead of watching the days slip by, awaiting his inevitable resignation, they embraced the time they had with him.

As I've said earlier, the security person you need today is not the one you need in two years' time. There is no harm in being honest about your plan to help your new leader do the best job they can in a short tenure, make a dent in the organisation's security action plan, and then be promoted or groomed for a new, more senior role. I believe every manager's job is to ready their staff for their next role and then set them free. If both parties are 'on the bus' with this, it's a very efficient, effective, and honest way to get the best outcomes for all involved. Planning for shorter tenure isn't for everyone, but, having said that, in 2016, the average Australian stayed in their job for just three years and four months, even less for millennials,[18] so it is not such a negative way to plan. We will talk in the next chapter about staff who stay for a long time, and the impact of this on both the candidate and their future in the organisation.

Key takeaway

Listen carefully in interviews when you ask the question *Where do you see yourself in five years' time?* This might seem like a corny, old-school question but it can tell you a lot about where the candidate sees all this going, if you're really listening to the hallmarks in their answer. Delve deeper with your questioning, if necessary, to find out what they need to stay for at least two years. If they are aspiring to be a CISO of a big company, for example, and you can't offer them this seniority, if such a role comes along, they may be enticed to greener pastures.

15

The expectation gap

'Greatness starts with a clear vision of the future.'

Simon Sinek, *author*

Your expectations, and those of the new leader, can be mostly addressed through the setting of your agenda (see chapter 2). With this documentation, the conversations you have had, and the right job description, it should be clear who you need to employ and what their outputs should be for the coming six, 12, or 18 months. Beyond that, they will need to create a broader strategy, but they will know that after their interview conversations with you.

Given the agenda setting, you should be able to limit any expectation gap in at least two of its variations: first, where the candidate believes they can achieve change and then falls flat because you haven't articulated what's possible in your specific environment; and, second, when an in-house candidate believes they can fulfil most of what the role or job description requires on paper but their history, background, and attitude preclude them. The following examples should clarify my point.

The excited new hire

About five years ago, I met a leader who arrived in the IT department new to the organisation, to the country, and to the industry – not new to IT but to the business's industry. He joined the organisation with dreams of pushing everything to the cloud, which he had done successfully in his previous role, innovating processes, and clearing out what he would identify as 'dead wood' among the staff. He reported for duty with gusto, raising his ideas at every opportunity, setting aside a budget for his grand plans, and genuinely planning disruption, which he believed was both possible and positive.

The shine soon came off his plans when the leadership team and his direct reports couldn't support his strategy. His grand plans didn't align with the regulations the business was required to adhere to, didn't fit with the old-school, risk-averse mentality of the organisation, and identifying 'dead wood' was not the way the business was run. None of these restrictions are necessarily right, but this was the way of the organisation, and a communication breakdown had occurred between the hiring manager and the new leader. There's a good chance that had he known his plans would fall on deaf ears, he would not have accepted the role.

It is so important to be clear what the new employee is walking into, what the boundaries might be, and if they (and you) feel they can deliver against everyone's expectations. Alternatively, if money and scope are no object, be clear about this lack of boundaries too. This can be a challenge for some people who like structure and are not blue-sky thinkers. Aim to set your new employee up for success by being clear on what is achievable.

The IT security manager who aspires to be head of information security

The second example is one I have seen on a number of occasions in mid-sized organisations that have been around for 10-plus years. In two almost identical cases, the organisations had an IT security policy manager (or similar title) whose role was to manage updates to security-related policies, enforce polices, exceptions, or exemptions to policies, and educate the staff on the existence and application of policies. This role was important and played a part in the business's audit compliance. The two managers each had at least 15 years' experience with their businesses, most of which had been in security or compliance. They were well connected, knew the business well, and were known for their role in compliance-type activities. Great, right? Yes. But these attributes and experiences were not necessarily leading them to a leadership/c-level role.

When their organisations were waking up to the new cyber threat and the risks being realised by organisations globally, audits ensued. These raised hundreds of concerns, one of which was a lack of leadership and visibility in the IT security area. It was not only a lack of leadership but of senior staff addressing cyber risk, and a concern that security was not recognised in executive conversations about projects, products, or initiatives. There was also the possibility that the organisations had suffered a cyber breach and didn't know it. Given that, in 2016, the average detection time to identify a cyber breach was 146 days globally, and 469 days for Europe, the Middle East, and Africa (EMEA),[19] you can understand why some heads have come up out of the sand in recent years, in relation to cyber.

The CIOs were asked to go out and find a senior cyber security leader, and the IT security manager/policy manager confidently submitted an expression of interest in the role. This person was qualified in many aspects of the job, but IT security (or cyber or information security) has changed over the past few years. And it continues to change. Security managers are often good writers, negotiators, technically sound, and well connected. However, they may also underestimate the jump from managing a structured, relatively black-and-white operation to what can be a roller-coaster ride as a head of cyber security or CISO.

Promoting from within can work, and I've written a few blogs about the benefits of internal staff complementing the security function with other skills. However, not all security experience is equal, and, in both cases, bringing in a fresh set of eyes with experience from other corners of the industry successfully addressed the cyber risk. (We will talk about measuring the impact of a new employee later.)

Both of these managers had great experience and provided value to the organisation through their loyalty, tenure, and vast knowledge of security. Supporting them in their current roles by the appointment of a leader to guide them into a new era of security was a good outcome for all involved. Promoting these managers would have been an easy way to address the audit findings, but was not in the best interest of the business.

Key takeaway

Be clear on what the candidate can achieve in the role, both in their aspirations and their abilities. It might seem too good to be true to have a motivated, enthusiastic candidate raring to go in the new role. But be mindful of whether you can harness that enthusiasm, and the impact this might have on the outcomes that need to be achieved.

Section 5

Coaching: Don't leave them high and dry

'We don't have to do it all alone. We were never meant to.'

Brené Brown, *scholar, author*

When it comes to first days on a job, mine have often involved people I already knew or had dealt with in the industry. This makes it easier to settle in, as you have some trust and rapport from the start.

I have also begun in organisations where I haven't seen my boss for the first few weeks. I've been handed a strategy, sometimes a team, and been left to my devices. This is daunting, especially when the organisation is large, or security is new and expectations are lacking.

This section talks about the value of your involvement as CIO with the new security leader from day one, some tips on their first few weeks and on how they might settle in. Further, it's about taking them through the agenda to give them a point of reference and help them with a starting point. They will always want to leave their mark on the strategy, and the agenda is merely a guiding light on where the fires are burning, so to speak. While helping the new employee settle in is the time to set expectations and remember some of the stretch you might have allowed for when committing to this leader.

Finally, when I titled this section 'Don't leave them high and dry', this extends past their cooling-off period. Bringing in a security leader takes ongoing effort. The best security roles I have had were when the CIO was active, taking part in the awareness campaigns, getting involved in the program of work, attending steering committee meetings, and asking tough questions. I'm not suggesting you smother them; neither do you need the burden of a leader who needs extensive hand holding. You want an expert, and you need to visibly support them.

This example might help to explain what I mean: I once helped an organisation to establish its agenda and find a head of cyber security. The organisation had a tradition that people would be given a black T-shirt with either a logo/emblem on it for certain projects or just with the company details on the front. Originally, it was planned that staff would wear the T-shirts to work to embrace the new branding, a small, visible, and tangible representation by those who wore the T-shirt that they could be counted on to represent the values of the organisation and didn't care who knew it. This marketing activity then turned into a saying that described employees who embraced and embodied the values of their business. Those who were committed, loyal, and focused on helping the company reach its objectives were often referred to colloquially as 'wearing the T-shirt'.

Over time, there have been rare T-shirts that were somewhat of a trophy, and old T-shirts that were respected. But no matter the T-shirt's detail, the embodying of the values in people's actions was what was key. I loved this, because it was simple for anyone at any level of the hierarchy to gain the basic company T-shirt (and then the special shirts, by being involved beyond their immediate job). The expression 'wear/s the T-shirt' could be said and everyone knew the expected behaviours. Of course, I ensured there was a special cyber security T-shirt.

So, when your new security leader arrives, be sure you're ready to 'wear the *security* T-shirt'.

16

Welcome

'There are no strangers here, only friends you haven't yet met.'

William Butler Yeats, *Irish poet*

In chapter 12 I raised the fact that just by reporting for duty, the new security manager begins to change the face of security for your organisation. This is true, and it is literally the beginning.

People have diverse needs. Everyone works slightly differently, and depending on the seniority of the new employee, you may have to alter your approach in their first few weeks with your organisation. But despite the diversity of needs, when it comes to security, the following is universal in organisations where a security leader is a new addition, and can also inform the process when they are to lead an established security function. Every one of the ideas below is an opportunity to spread the security word, support your new leader, and open them up to assess different areas of the organisation. One of the main traits found among security professionals is their curious nature and sense of security when meeting new people and hearing about how different departments and products work together. Some of the below might seem obvious, while others might spark an idea.

1. **Set the tone.** The way this leader enters the business could set the tone for their relationship with you and the organisation. Giving them an hour of your time on their first day to reiterate your support, introduce them, set up some meetings, and get

the ball rolling is essential. This might seem obvious, but not all leaders operate in this way. Others see the first few weeks as a time for inhaling security and business literature, getting through induction (see number 5) and settling in. These are all important, but don't detract from that first day, when certainty and confidence can't be overdone. Whenever the tone was set on day one, I would re-read those day-one notes time and again – the first few pages of my notebook in a new role have proven so valuable. Having said that, it depends on whom you hire and what they need. Consider their needs, or ask them if they want the time to settle or to dive straight in. I've had bosses on both sides of this argument. While my preference is not to be left to my own devices, find out how your leader wants their first few days to play out.

2. **Introduce them.** Again, this might seem basic, but as the boss of a security leader, this is your first opportunity to show your support for this person and what they are there for. By all means ask them to write a blurb about themselves, but this introduction has a dual purpose in also reminding your workforce about security. Most people like to read about the new person, but if you can use their arrival to increase security knowledge or remind staff of its importance – in a light-hearted, culturally appropriate manner – take advantage of this situation. In addition to written communications, take the new person to meetings and send them to head office/ locations/parent companies to meet people. Introducing them lets the organisation know the security leader is there, and that they have a key role to play.

3. **Cup-of-tea tour.** Ask your assistant – and given that assistants are an endangered species, this might mean you – to set up a few coffee meetings with key stakeholders. Do not include vendors of any description. It needs to be only a few key people to kick-start important relationships. It might be

worth selecting some yourself, but also find out who from the executive team wants to proactively meet the new security leader. You may be surprised at who comes forward, keen to share their insights and needs. The new leader can, of course, do this for themselves, but if you begin the process, it is yet another opportunity for you to promote the security program.

4. **Buddy/mentor.** There are many variables that may make this one either troublesome or redundant, but it's worth mentioning. Depending on the size and age of the organisation, having someone who can answer some questions for the new leader is helpful, someone who may have been around for a while or who has seen change in the organisation who can brief the new leader when they need information. There are risks in this, that too much information from one source can be skewed. Also, if it's a start-up, it might be a small team/environment where anyone can service questions/needs. There are too many variables to discuss here, but it's worth considering having someone on hand to answer day-to-day inquiries when you are not available. This need also might be covered when you brief them on the agenda (see chapter 17), which could be sufficient information for the leader to start with.

5. **Onboarding.** Onboarding, or induction, is often forgotten when a new employee is quite senior. I have found the onboarding process tells me a lot about an organisation and what it sees as paramount for new staff to know. Things such as 'Is security/privacy covered, and to what extent?' are gold for a new security leader, especially if one of the 'big rocks' in the agenda is employee security awareness. The new employee can see where security might fit. Just because they are a senior leader, don't discount the value of their attendance at induction/onboarding days.

6. **Continued support ('wear the T-shirt').** See every opportunity to promote the security leader and their program. Support doesn't come only in the form of 1:1s, decisions, and budget. Support also needs to be visible to the rest of the organisation throughout projects, incidents, and when addressing boards and risk committees.

Key takeaway

If security is new to your organisation, it's impossible to set and forget and still expect good outcomes and retention from this leader. Security roles are a hard slog, and they need support from you and all stakeholders to keep the program afloat. Take every opportunity you can to involve yourself from day one in visible support for the leader and what they are doing to contribute to the organisation and protect your customers.

17

Update

*'Make visible what, without you,
might perhaps never have been seen.'*

Robert Bresson, *French film director*

Chapters 17 and 18 go hand in hand. Updating the new security leader on the agenda and setting your expectations are integral to their success.

In previous chapters we talked about the importance of the agenda and how working through the notes taken and establishing the three main areas of focus (big rocks) are important for the new leader.

Chances are that they will have their own ideas based on where they came from and where they want their experience to take them. And this is fine. The agenda is a great starting point for them to understand what the leaders think, and upon which to build their strategy. But since the agenda was written, leaders might have changed and directions altered, so the new leader will need to be briefed not only on the agenda but on any changes, big and small, since the agenda was agreed.

In one organisation I worked with, between the agenda being finalised and the new leader starting, there was a significant change not only in the c-suite but in the next level of management too. A new position of chief operating officer was created, new executive leaders were hired for departments such as customer service, engineering, employee experience, and the legal team all experienced changes. With this comes direction changes and strategic reviews as the new leaders settle in. This shouldn't change the big rocks as such, but it's worth understanding those who have exited and the influence they might have had on the agenda. For example, a big rock might have been locking down security with third parties through contracts. If you don't have access to lawyers to review contracts, one of your big rocks might become less achievable in the short term. Similarly, if one of your big rocks is application security, and the head of engineering or development and operations changes, they will want to understand their workforce and systems before agreeing to security-related changes. Changes in the c-suite will affect not only the agenda but perhaps your role as CIO, something to be aware of if your new security leader arrives amidst significant organisational change.

Some other potential changes that could occur between the agenda being finalised and the new staff member's arrival that you might want to brief them on might include:

- cost cutting
- restructures
- outsourcing
- shifts from on-premise to cloud
- security-related incidents, their impact, resolution, and lessons learnt
- new threats based on security events within the industry
- new audit findings
- new operating models

As CIO, you don't need to conduct all these update briefings. It may be that as the new leader meets people across the organisation, those people can fill in the blanks and provide updates. The key is to consider this information, as it's an important change from the content they read in the agenda. Similarly, if you have some audit remediation already underway, have someone brief the new leader on how it is occurring, who the responsible parties are, and what role the new leader may play in collaborating with the auditors on security-focused items.

Key takeaway

In addition to the agenda briefing, an update on changes in the organisation and anything that affects the big rocks significantly is important. Assumptions that the agenda reflects the current state of the organisation can be dangerous if some time has passed, and getting the security leader off on the right foot with key stakeholders is a priority.

18

What is coaching? (It's not about screaming from the sidelines)

'Coaching is unlocking people's potential to maximise their own performance.'

John Whitmore, *executive coaching pioneer*

Part of transitioning your new employee to the organisation may involve the use of a coach. This investment is helpful on a number of fronts, especially considering the details we covered in the previous chapter. Coaching can assist in thinking about innovative ways to deliver more secure outcomes to an organisation that might not, until now, have had anyone address cyber risk.

Having been a mentor, and having talked a great deal to peers, direct reports, executives, and people in general, I thought I knew what coaching was before I earned my coaching accreditation – how it was valuable and why people might seek it out. But you know what they say about assumptions. It turned out that some of my preconceived ideas were wrong. In reality, coaching is a lot about the coach formulating great questions, then piping down, listening, and creating enough trust and tension to steer their client into useful outcomes.

The International Coaching Federation defines it as 'an ongoing professional relationship that helps people produce extraordinary results in their lives, careers, businesses or organisations. Through the process of coaching, clients deepen their learning, improve their performance, and enhance their quality of life.'[20]

So why am I telling you this, and why would your new hire need a coach? Because even if they're killing it, there is always room for improvement. (We will talk about 'addressing the stretch' in chapter 20, which is a good time to use a coach.) You may have dismissed the idea of providing coaching for your staff because of cost or because you think it's your role to coach your direct reports through issues, concerns, and complex decisions. However, some of the most successful people in the world have coaches who specialise in their field, and many have engaged a coach even though they were already successful. Coaching is about developing the capabilities of high-potential performers. Coaching works for those who are willing to learn, grow, and be accountable for their future. Coaching in one's career or personal life is no different to elite athletes working with their coach to improve on already world-class results.

In the case of hiring and retaining cyber security talent, coaching helps individuals transition into their roles, work through complex problems that might come up, and enhance the way they perform.

Depending on the agreed goals and outcomes you have set when working through section 5 of this book's framework, the following types of things can be explored during coaching sessions:

- Role-play scenarios: practising and experimenting with possible responses to anticipated situations to polish skills and build comfort with new behaviours
- Creating better listening and questioning skills to improve delivery against stakeholder expectations
- Problem solving: stimulating creative problem solving by asking probing questions
- Brainstorming solutions to real work challenges

Coaching supports new employees, increases retention, builds commitment and, unlike mentoring, encourages the leader to discover their own solutions and deliver results. Joining an organisation as the only security leader can be empowering but also isolating. Providing your leader with the opportunity to work through some of the challenges with a coach in the early months, and periodically in the future, can be of enormous value to the organisation.

Key takeaway

Coaching isn't mentoring, counselling, managing, or directing. Coaching is a valuable resource for the new employee to assist their transition, work through options, and address behaviours that might hold them back or paralyse them in their new role. A coach allows your leader to build confidence by arriving at their own list of options, which they can assess with you as CIO. Empower your new leader to choose a coach they have rapport with and that you are comfortable possesses the legitimate skills.

19

What does the candidate need?

'Supporting another's success won't ever dampen yours.'

Anonymous

Below are some suggestions of things that have worked for me and others in the industry when starting out in a new role or during my tenure. As a security leader, all support is welcome and appreciated. There are many ways to support the new leader, and while I spoke about these in chapter 16 in the short term, of their first 30 days, here are a few longer-term needs.

They need quality third-party consultants

During my research, one of the CIOs suggested that if the head of information security role sat empty for a long time – fortunately, in his case, it didn't – he would bring in a consultant to tide over the organisation while it found the leader it wanted. This is what he had done in 2015, even though the organisation had found someone to take the role advertised. The role was empty for six weeks, and yet, as soon as the incumbent had resigned, a consultant was brought in to manage the potential gap. At the time of writing (2017), that consultant is still there, despite the team now comprising five strong security specialists.

The consultant's current role is to support larger security projects, provide day-to-day generalist advice, and keep the business up to date on what he sees in security across other clients within his consulting company. This CIO is not the first person to keep a security consultant on long after the new leader has joined. It is recognised that they can't do it alone, and yet, getting budget for teams is a challenge. Obtaining funding for a consultant is a little easier. Their knowledge is also fresh, and despite the risk that they might not be permanent, there is value in their ability to deliver what the new leader needs from a second pair of expert hands.

They need budget and tools

I won't bang on too long about budget and tools, mostly because I'm all about the people in security, however, I will say this: In 2016, SANS[21] undertook research into security budgets, most of which were within IT expenditure. Protection of sensitive information and regulatory compliance are the two most significant business drivers behind security spending. Bringing in a security leader is not the start, middle, and end of your expenses. To achieve great things, your new leader potentially needs funding for automation tools, third-party assessments, detection and monitoring tools, testing, compliance-related systems, and cloud-based security applications (think distributed denial of service (DDOS) and hosting). Staff training, certification, and keeping up to date through conferences and courses also cost money. If you plan to make security a business priority, you must reflect this in your budget – to not just borrow from Peter to pay Paul but truly allocate security spend. Getting the budget you need requires more than measuring the success of past investment, which might have been very little in security, or masked by dual-purpose (security and IT combined) hardware and services. It also revolves around ensuring compliance, enabling business objectives, and providing proof of improvements in incident counts and risk profile, the top four justification points used in obtaining a security budget, according to SANS respondents.[22]

They need exposure

It's unlikely that a trip to the board or audit committee is high on your agenda for your new security leader in their first 30 days. However, it is worth planning for this to happen sooner rather than later. One of the CIOs I spoke with suggested that despite the new security leader, he still saw his role as the educator of the board on all things security. This approach can work fine day to day, but when there is a breach or an incident, the board needs to know the person who is managing the risk/issue/incident/impact. Meeting them for the first time during an incident isn't ideal.

With global cyber events on the rise, I wonder how many boards have recently met their security leaders for the first time, or after a long hiatus between updates. Boards are made up of people – who are only human – whose concerns branch from uncertainty and a lack of information. The security leader can increase their knowledge about the state of security affairs, provide a regular, valid, and business-relevant update, a clear view of the risk, and your plans to minimise and mitigate such threats. You want to provide certainty that cyber risk is being addressed, and for the board to build trust in your security leader.

If the board is already across your cyber security strategy, including your approach when incidents arise, this ensures that any urgent board meetings about a cyber event will be more focused on the task at hand. Many organisations include cyber risk in their corporate risk registers – often at No. 1 – but not all 'socialise the strategy' on how this risk is being addressed up to board level. Regular, engaging strategic updates are key, so that when incidents happen, the board already knows the security leader and the progress towards improving security maturity.

In the 2016 Australian Cyber Security Centre Survey, it was found that its more cyber-resilient respondents were 'far more likely to have discussed cyber security at the board level within the last three months (87%) compared with those categorised as less resilient (59%)'.[23]

The survey also revealed that in less cyber-resilient organisations, 21% of recent board-level cyber security discussions were prompted by an incident, compared with just 6% for more resilient organisations. Additionally, less resilient organisations were generally more likely than others to reactively discuss cyber security.

The report also said that 'regardless of resilience, more needs to be done to embed cyber security into the core strategic business of senior management'.

Overall, in 27% of respondents, cyber security is rarely, if ever, discussed at the most senior level. Now is the time to bring security into the boardroom, if it has not already been introduced. Involvement of senior management in cyber security discussions is a leading factor in successfully mitigating cyber security risks. 'Ultimately, better understanding by senior decision makers of cyber security helps organisations respond to incidents more effectively.'[24]

In time, your new leader might need a team

All businesses have to start somewhere in focusing on security, and a new security leader is a great place to begin. It does wonders for the organisation's commitment to security to have someone dedicated to reducing the risks. But, as I mentioned earlier, security leaders cannot do this alone, and while consultants can be helpful at times, the need to protect your organisation can be fulfilled only by specialists who can sit in the business and meet its needs, especially if the business is growing.

When I arrived at Sportsbet, it was just me and a third-party consultant who had been there a few months. By the time I left, a year later, there was an application security specialist, an architect, an analyst, and a head of information security to replace me. Sportsbet was a 700-strong organisation that took every hour the security team could give them, thanks to a strong commitment to security. This was, and is, an organisation committed to supporting its security team, meeting regulatory obligations – which requires resources – and reducing audit findings to a minimum. This couldn't be done without an expert team working closely with the business on technologies (new and old), delving into new initiatives, increasing the knowledge of others, and raising the security bar.

What the candidate doesn't need

Some of this is reiteration, but for completeness, let's look at a handful of things a security leader doesn't need or want or have the skills to manage.

- Your new security leader is not the new owner of every audit finding/action for the whole business for the rest of time, or for those stray findings that haven't seen the light of day since before the war. Yes, audit findings often lead to management commitments based on new or improved security controls, but a lot of audit findings have nothing to do with information/ cyber security. Please ensure that the new leader doesn't get lumped with managing IT's audit findings, which often happens because security is perceived as a close partner of audit.
- Your new leader can't be all things to all people. It's become apparent from security job ads that most security people are required to be a jack of all trades. Compliance people need also to be security people. Or the fraud guy must double as the information security leader. Or the head of information security must also analyse the security event logs. Businesses often mistakenly seek one person to solve all of their security problems. It seems like common sense to point out that one person can't fill the roles of many, but with many of the jobs advertised today, it seems that is the expectation.
- They don't need security vendor introductions for at least the first six months. Salespeople are great at what they do, but chances are the security leader won't know enough about the network and the business operations to add value to a discussion. Furthermore, most security leaders would prefer

to contact vendors when they need them, based on the strategy they deliver.

- They don't need to take ownership of activities or outcomes that should be managed by the business. I mentioned this above, about audit, but there are also tasks that businesses sometimes wrongly look to cyber security to own; for example, third-party vendor engagement. The security team is responsible for providing a list of requirements that third parties must meet to logically or physically connect with your network. Security doesn't need to own the risk or the final decision on whether to engage with the vendor. Legal, IT, compliance, and finance can all play a part in signing off or advising on the risks involved with a particular vendor. If the business takes all the advice and wants to accept the risk, that may be fine by the security team. Consider the real owner of risk-reduction processes before assigning cyber/information security staff to own them.

This list, as with all others in this book, is by no means exhaustive.

Key takeaway

A new security leader will need more than day-to-day support from you. They need to feel confident that their purpose is clear, that they have been budgeted and planned for, and that their input will be valued.

20

Addressing the stretch

'We rise by lifting others.'

Robert G. Ingersoll, *lawyer, US Civil War veteran*

In all the roles I have taken on, and I'm sure most people would say the same, there has been somewhat of a stretch for me from day one to achieve what was desired. We talked in chapter 18 about expectations, and part of the new leader delivering on these will be your commitment to 'addressing the stretch'.

When I first led a trust and safety team 10 years ago, my stretch was evident. I had never led fraud analysts before, they were in the throes of choosing and integrating a multimillion-dollar fraud detection tool and I had no idea how it worked, and I had never been exposed to ecommerce security before. I entered this role after working in corporate security, building up expertise in dealing with law enforcement. I knew little about dealing with commercial staff or security vendors.

I had been tapped on the shoulder for this role by someone I had worked with a number of years before, and the management team were content with my skill set. The team I landed with were great analysts and hard workers who knew their craft and needed only my leadership and support to ensure fraud prevention was part of project discussions and product planning. This I could do. But to address the stretch, I undertook to widen my skills and knowledge myself. I sought experts from around the business to support my integration with the organisation. I learnt how an ecommerce platform worked, sat with the analysts to understand how online fraud worked – and how to prevent it – and built a network of supporters around me to help fill the gaps in my knowledge.

What I learnt in this role was that I had many transferable skills, my love of people management kept my days buoyant, and I believed in the product and protecting the customers who used it. While my boss didn't involve himself in my upskilling, this meant that it took a little longer to address the stretch, and I leant heavily on the support of those around me to prepare me for the broader, bolder roles ahead.

I recently asked a friend, whom I'll call David, about his experience with a CIO supporting him to address the stretch. David's time in the security industry was in utilities in the mid-2000s, and during a period of extensive IT transformation, an interim CIO was brought in to recruit the permanent CIO and implement the new IT organisational structure. One of those roles was the head of information security.

At the time, David was a business analyst, working four layers down from the CIO in the IT department. He was in his mid-twenties and had a Master's degree in Information Systems. He was passionate about being involved in this IT transformation.

David met regularly with the interim CIO to advise him on work completed by the transformation team. In one meeting, the CIO asked David for his views on information security, disaster recovery, and business continuity planning. A few days later he was appointed head of information security, with responsibility for disaster recovery and business continuity planning. He was to start immediately and report directly to the CIO. Overnight, David had been elevated three levels and was accountable for domains, of which he had no experience. Risky, right?

Over the ensuing months, the acting CIO mentored David into the role. He was given freedom and encouraged to make big decisions. The support was simple, but powerful, and David embraced the opportunity he had been given. David's view was constantly being challenged until the CIO was comfortable with the decisions being made. He was also allowed to make some mistakes, as long as he demonstrated he had learnt from them.

Taking a chance on a leader is an amazing gesture, but it also involves a lot of hard work in terms of coaching and mentoring. In David's case, the CIO gave him the autonomy he needed to make mistakes and grow, and provided enough guidance and support to minimise those mistakes over time.

Unfortunately, in some cases, people are appointed with the best of intentions but circumstances change. For example, recently, a CIO I spoke with had internally appointed a security leader, moving an infrastructure leader to the security role with plans to support him in his transition. He had been with the organisation a long time, had the respect of management, and in the eyes of the CIO, could handle the new responsibility. He was not her first choice, as he lacked a strong security background, but she was willing to mentor him and support his needs in addressing the stretch.

Due to unforeseen circumstances, the CIO left the organisation a few months later, so she was no longer there to mentor the leader in his new role. How the organisation managed this would be crucial to the security function, and to how security was perceived within IT and the broader business. The CIO's exit could not have been predicted. Therefore, it's vital that the CIO ensure that the head of information security has the support of other executives and can seek the support of the incoming CIO to ensure the ongoing protection of the organisation.

Key takeaway

Addressing the stretch in your new security leader's skill set can be a rewarding and rich experience for both of you. Even if your new leader doesn't require extensive support or improvement, your committed backing will go a long way to retaining their talent. If they come into the role with a large amount of room for growth, be sure they are a willing participant in their upskilling. This is key to the evolution of a well-rounded leader and the success of the security function.

21

Where to from here?
A word on measurement

'If you can't measure it, you can't improve it.'

Peter F. Drucker, *author*

It's been said that you get what you measure. This is certainly true of security, and even more so, one hopes, true of your new employee. Thinking about how all the hard work you have put into hiring, establishing the agenda, and setting your expectations can be proved a success is one of the most important parts of establishing your new security leader.

According to LinkedIn's 2016 global trends report, the quality of the person hired is a priority for 40% of large companies and 45% of smaller ones.[25] But how many of these businesses actually measure the quality of their new employee? Traditionally, security roles were considered difficult to evaluate based on the measurements you might assume appropriate, measurements such as zero breaches, or zero data lost, or zero security incidents. But incidents, breaches, and data loss cannot be completely controlled. Don't confuse measuring your leader with measuring the program. Measuring whether your hire has met your expectations can be based on your agenda, what you want the leader to achieve against broader business key performance indicators, and how they might be progressing in addressing the stretch.

Basic measurement can be achieved with the following guidelines:

- Be specific. If you want them to deliver the agenda objectives within six months, ensure they can break this down into achievable chunks, with clear numbers and/or expectations agreed.
- Create realistic deadlines based on what can be achieved considering other staff activities, those who might need to help, and funding. For example, if your aim is to implement automated secure code testing, this can be a large investment and involve tendering or negotiating with vendors, training all developers, writing secure code guidelines, and socialising the changes that might affect delivery frameworks. This is a huge task that may not be achievable within a short deadline if the leader is working alone. (See the next point about being realistic.)
- Be realistic. Set goals that can be achieved with stretch targets on top, if that will help the leader grow (and the stretch remains realistic).
- Be clear. Write the measurements/goals so that an outsider reading it would be clear about exactly what is expected and why.
- Evaluate the what, why, and how of the leader. If they achieve everything you set for them in the first six months, but they do it with aggression or struggle, then it's not necessarily successful against your non-negotiables, culture fit, or objectives for this leader.
- Listen to the leader's suggestions on how they can be measured, and incorporate these ideas.

There are a number of other things to consider when measuring success. Asking yourself the following questions, in no particular order, can help to establish some of the measures above:

1. Who is judging the success?

2. Returning to your plans from chapter 2, what were you planning to achieve by hiring this leader in the short to medium term?

3. Should the employee be part of setting the assessment criteria as well?

4. What is your minimum expectation of delivery?

5. When will you know it's been a success?

6. What are others saying about the new hire and the progress they see?

7. What role will you play in the success of the new employee?

8. What will you do if the new hire doesn't meet your expectations?

9. What other resources might be available to you to address any concerns?

Part of the success of a new employee is down to you. I have had both successes and times when I wish things had gone differently. In both cases, it came down to the level of my preparation before hiring. In the case where it could have been better, I had brought in a new leader to report to me, and, a few weeks in, he approached me and explained his concerns about the role and the organisation, as he didn't have a clear view of his purpose. The role was newly created, and I, too, didn't have a clear view of where his role should go in the first few months, let alone what he could expect to achieve. I had expectations, but these were just the bare bones, with no meat on them. We were a great fit, culturally, and got along well in terms of my management and his delivery style. However, it was only when I sat down and set clear KPIs (key performance indicators) with him did he gain a sense of achievement and I began to see great results. I learnt a lot from this experience, and would not want to see other leaders in a similar position, especially when some new employees do not necessarily feel confident to step forward and admit they don't see a clear path ahead. Part of his challenge was a value misalignment with the organisation, which also clouded his day-to-day judgement. (We covered this in section 5, but I'm highlighting it again because its importance shouldn't be underestimated.)

Keeping a close eye on your interactions with your new leader will help you to measure the quality of your hiring decision. Where necessary, leverage coaching opportunities with a third-party coach for an independent perspective, understand what the appointee needs, and be realistic about the ecosystem they are becoming part of. This can help them not only to settle into the role but to understand the risks better, and meet broader expectations.

Key takeaway

Taking your new leader on this journey of measurement can set the precedent for their hiring of other security staff who come into the organisation under their umbrella. And while this book suggests a framework when hiring security professionals and leaders, it can also serve as a reminder that no matter whom you hire, doing the hard thinking and planning first can make for a much more confident hiring decision for you, and a higher likelihood that you'll retain the staff member.

22

It's never a 'wrap'

'What feels like the end is often the beginning.'

Anonymous

Movie directors will shout, 'That's a wrap', when filming is complete. Once done, it's up to another team of experts to come in, take the hard work of the actors, and create a movie that will win box office acclaim.

When it comes to hiring and retaining cyber security talent, it's never a wrap. You can't set and forget these people. You can't afford to imagine they will be able to function without support. Aside from the probable need for more security staff around them, there's a real chance that some of their peers in the organisation will require coaxing to support the security function, especially if it's new.

Many organisations travel along in quiet ignorance about their security position – remember, the average time to detect a breach is more than 140 days. So, the introduction of this staff member may seem more like an interruption rather than a welcome change to the IT leadership team.

The new leader will likely feel overwhelmed when they first join. And after the initial flurry of activity – greeting the executive team, bedding down the strategy, and kicking off the regular security-related meetings – the hard work certainly lies ahead of them.

I have had heads of cyber security call me weeks into a new role, concerned that they are not the right fit, that they can't keep up with the organisation's rapid delivery on customer expectations, or they feel they can't achieve the strategy on their own. Others call me every six months when they find themselves in the same position as their organisation goes through the ebbs and flows of delivery, budgets, project delays, and breaches. I coach these leaders regarding their value and remind newer employees that trust and impact take time, that they don't want to be labelled as that person who came in and slammed the table to make the chess pieces all fall down, figuratively speaking.

As a CIO, your role as a mentor and a business leader is important. We discussed at the very beginning about how every CIO's workload is growing, you're becoming more strategic, and you have more than ever on your plate. I'm not suggesting that the new security leader is, or will be, needy. What I am suggesting is that even if you don't know a lot about security and can't offer subject matter guidance, your new leader will likely need your support to rally the troops and raise the profile of security initially as well as in the longer term.

One CIO I interviewed suggested the security know-how of a CIO was more important when assessing a potential candidate than the security maturity of the organisation. He believed the ability of the CIO to support the security leader, and their reliance on that security leader to educate them, was key. This suggests to me that the CIO needs just as much support and guidance, especially in the early days, as the security leader does.

It may seem that the hiring and retaining a cyber security leader is a lot of hard work, and it can be. But with careful planning it can also be rewarding, and can shape you into a more rounded CIO with excellent experience to take into future roles.

Valuable references/links

Australian Information Security Association
www.aisa.org.au

Australian Women in Security Network
https://www.auswomeninsecurity.net

Department of the Prime Minister and Cabinet, Australia
https://www.pmc.gov.au/cyber-security

Security Job Profile Project
https://www.securityjobprofileproject.com

Australian Cyber Security Centre
https://www.acsc.gov.au

The SANS Institute (information security training
and certification)
https://www.sans.org/reading-room/whitepapers/analyst/
security-spending-trends-36697

The Australian Cyber Security Skills Shortage Study 2016
https://www.aisa.org.au/Public/Training_Pages/Research/
AISA%20Cyber%20security%20skills%20shortage%20
research.aspx

Cybersec People
https://www.cybersecpeople.com

Decipher Bureau
https://www.decipherbureau.com

Q1 Recruitment
https://q1group.com.au

ISACA (formerly, Information Systems Audit and Control Association)
http://www.isaca.org.au

Cloud Security Alliance
https://cloudsecurityalliance.org

Acknowledgements

This book would not have been possible without the support of the KPI community, Andrew Griffiths, and my accountability group (Jordan, Susie, Lalita, and Kate) who provide consistant inspiration, feedback, and enthusiasm for my goals.

I am especially indebted to those CIOs, my industry peers, and the members of the Australian Women in Security Network who have validated my ideas, contributed to my research, and actively provided me with the motivation, assistance, and case studies needed to support my writing.

I would like to thank my parents and siblings; whose love and guidance are with me in whatever I pursue.

Most importantly, I wish to thank my loving husband, Wayne, and our four children – my cheer squad. To have published a book during one of our most challenging, yet exciting years to date is certainly only due to your encouragement and the belief you have in me.

Notes

1. Liam Tung, 'Q3 2017 report: there's 2,200 percent more malicious email than last year', CSO Online, 27 October 2017, https://www.cso.com.au/article/629171/q3-2017-report-there-2-200-percent-more-malicious-email-than-last-year/.

2. Barbara Filkins, 'IT Security Spending Trends: a SANS Survey, SANS Institute, February 2016, https://www.sans.org/reading-room/whitepapers/analyst/security-spending-trends-36697

3. Ibid.

4. 2016 Cyber Security Survey, Australian Cyber Security Centre, Australian Government, https://www.acsc.gov.au/publications/ACSC_Cyber_Security_Survey_2016.pdf.

5. Ibid.

6. Ibid.

7. Maria Korolov, 'Look beyond job boards to fill cybersecurity roles', CSO Online, IDG Communications, 13 July 2017, https://www.csoonline.com/article/3206688/it-careers/firms-look-beyond-job-boards-to-find-and-recruit-cybersecurity-talent.html.

8. 'The Australian Cyber Security Skills Shortage Study 2016', AISA Research Report, Australian Information Security Association, https://www.agix.com.au/wp-content/uploads/2016/12/AISA-skills-shortage.pdf.

9. Ibid.

10. 'Challenges to Australia's Cyber Security Industry, Australian Cyber Security Growth Network, April 2017, https://www.acsgn.com/cyber-security-sector-competitiveness-plan/challenges-australias-cyber-security-industry/.

11. Patrick Howell O'Neill, 'Women paid less than men at every level of cybersecurity industry, report says', Cyberscoop, 15 March 2017, https://www.cyberscoop.com/women-in-cybersecurity-wage-gap-report/.

12. The only time this changes is if a major breach has occurred and securing the organisation is the immediate strategy for the foreseeable future.

13. Heather Ricciuto, 'Representation of Woman in Cybersecurity Remains Stagnant, Despite Recent Efforts to Balance the Scales', Security Intelligence, IBM, 15 March 2017, https://securityintelligence.com/representation-of-women-in-cybersecurity-remains-stagnant-despite-recent-efforts-to-balance-the-scales/.

14. Ricciuto, 'Representation of Woman in Cybersecurity Remains Stagnant, Despite Recent Efforts to Balance the Scales', 15 March 2017, https://securityintelligence.com/representation-of-women-in-cybersecurity-remains-stagnant-despite-recent-efforts-to-balance-the-scales/.

15. Megan Noel, 'Why women don't apply for jobs they're not 100% qualified for (but should), The American Genius, 23 February 2016, https://theamericangenius.com /business-news/women-apply-for-jobs/.

16. Gina Belli, 'At least 70% of jobs are not even listed – here's how to up your chances of getting a great new gig', Business Insider, 10 April 2017, http://www.businessinsider.com/at-least-70-of-jobs-are-not-even-listed-heres-how-to-up-your-chances-of-getting-a-great-new-gig-2017-4?IR=T.

17. Vincent S. Flowers & Charles L. Hughes, 'Why Employees Stay', Harvard Business Review, July 1973 issue, https://hbr.org/1973/07/why-employees-stay.

18. Ben Phillips, 'Is the "job for life" mentality gone for good?' Adzuna's Blog, 4 February 2016, https://www.adzuna.com.au/blog/2016/02/04/is-the-job-for-life-mentality-gone-for-good/.

19. Chris Gerritz, 'Breach Detection by the Numbers: Days, Weeks or Years?', Infocyte, 27 July 2016, https://www.infocyte.com/blog/2016/7/26/how-many-days-does-it-take-to-discover-a-breach-the-answer-may-shock-you. See also Herb Weisbaum, 'Data Breaches Happening at Record Pace, Report Finds', NBC Business News, 24 July 2017, https://www.nbcnews.com/business/consumer/data-breaches-happening-record-pace-report-finds-n785881.

20. International Coach Federation, Coaching FAQs, https://www.coachfederation.org/need/landing.cfm?ItemNumber=978.

21. Barbara Filkins, 'IT Security Spending Trends', Survey, SANS Institute, February 2016, https://www.sans.org/reading-room/whitepapers/analyst/security-spending-trends-36697.

22. Ibid.

23. 2016 Cyber Security Survey, Australian Cyber Security Centre, Australian Government, 2017, https://www.acsc.gov.au/publications/ACSC_Cyber_Security_Survey_2016.pdf.

24. Ibid.

25. Nikolette Zika, 'How to measure the quality of hire', Workable (n.d.), https://resources.workable.com/blog/quality-of-hire

26. Gerritz, 'Breach Detection by the Numbers', https://www.infocyte.com/blog/2016/7/26/how-many-days-does-it-take-to-discover-a-breach-the-answer-may-shock-you. See also Weisbaum, 'Data Breaches Happening at Record Pace,' https://www.nbcnews.com/business/consumer/data-breaches-happening-record-pace-report-finds-n785881.

www.ingramcontent.com/pod-product-compliance
Lightning Source LLC
Chambersburg PA
CBHW071254050326
40690CB00011B/2393